The Official Family Tree Maker® 9

fast&easy®

The Official Family Tree Maker® 9

fast&easy®

Rhonda R. McClure

Premier
Press

Premier

Press Premier Press is a registered trademark of Premier Press, Inc.

Publisher: Stacy L. Hiquet

Associate Marketing Manager: Heather Buzzingham

Managing Editor: Sandy Doell

Acquisitions Editor: Emi Smith

Project Editor: Cathleen D. Snyder

Technical Reviewer: Amy Johnson Crow

Copy Editor: Laura R. Gabler

Interior Layout: Shawn Morningstar

Cover Design: Mike Tanamachi

ISBN: 1-931841-02-0

Library of Congress Catalog Card Number: 2001091384

Printed in the United States of America

01 02 03 04 DD 10 9 8 7 6 5 4 3 2 1

For Rhody and Carnie, I love you both

Acknowledgments

An author is but one facet to a good book. There are many people who work hard to ensure that the final product is nothing but the best. Without these helpful people this book would not be the useful resource that you now hold. To Emi Smith, thank you for the chance to work with you and Premier Press again. A thank you to Cathleen Snyder, whose eye and approach helped to make the chapters their best. Appreciation to Laura R. Gabler for her copy editing. A hearty thank you to Amy Johnson Crow, a tech editor who keeps me honest. Finally, special thanks to Brian Bond of Genealogy.com who, despite the pressures of getting this product out the door, took the time to answer my questions about the new features.

About the Author

Rhonda R. McClure has managed to combine the best of both worlds—computers and genealogy. She has been using a computer to aid in her genealogical research since 1985. She has been teaching genealogists for over 10 years on the benefits of their genealogy software—a time-saving addition to their research when understood. She can be found at national conferences, guiding genealogists to an understanding of Family Tree Maker. This is Rhonda's second book; she was the author of *Family Tree Maker 8 Fast & Easy: The Official Guide* (Prima Tech, 2000).

Contents at a Glance

Contents

PART VI
ADVANCED FAMILY TREE MAKER METHODS **333**

Introduction

This Fast & Easy book from Premier Press will help you learn Family Tree Maker 9 so you can spend more of your time researching your family history and less time entering it into a program. Family Tree Maker is a multi-faceted program able not only to track your ancestry, but also to produce beautiful reports for sharing what you find. Even if you have never used a genealogy program before, you will find that Family Tree Maker's interface and options make it possible to track even the most tangled of family trees. With the capability to include digitized images, Family Tree Maker gives you the opportunity to share more than just dry names, dates, and places. This book introduces you to many of the features available in Family Tree Maker so you can enjoy this hobby you've discovered. Even if you've used Family Tree Maker before, you might find some new tricks in Part VI, "Advanced Family Tree Maker Methods."

Who Should Read this Book

This book is written with the novice computer user in mind. In it, you are taken on a hands-on trip through the Family Tree Maker program. The many illustrations let you check your progress as you master each new feature or process. Even if you are familiar with computers, though, you might have only recently been introduced to Family Tree Maker. In either case, this book offers you an easy-to-follow tour of the program and all that you can accomplish. Finally, those who feel comfortable with the basic features of Family Tree Maker might find some shortcuts or new methods for working with the program.

This book is organized by tasks. Some tasks require many steps, and others branch off into enhancements or additional features. A quick perusal of the Table of Contents should lead you right to the process you are trying to accomplish. Then it is just a matter of reading through the steps.

Special Features of this Book

As you work with this book, you will discover that the emphasis is on tasks. This is by design, so that you can master the skills in an easy-to-follow format. There are a couple of features, though, that will supply you with additional information as you work with the Family Tree Maker program.

TIP

Tips offer useful hints about features in Family Tree Maker that can speed up the task at hand or enhance your report output.

NOTE

Notes offer additional information about the Family Tree Maker program, or about genealogy and sharing your family tree in general.

CAUTION

Cautions warn you of potential problems that might occur when you are working with your family tree.

In the appendixes, you will find instructions on installing the Family Tree Maker software, as well as useful tables of keyboard shortcuts to make your data entry speedier.

Happy family tree climbing!

PART I

Introduction to Family Tree Maker

1

Getting Started with Family Tree Maker

Before you can take advantage of the many features of Family Tree Maker, you must first know how to launch or open it. You must then have some information about your family history to enter into it. Family Tree Maker offers different methods for both opening the program and beginning a new Family File. In this chapter, you'll learn how to:

- Start Family Tree Maker using the menu
- Start Family Tree Maker using the desktop icon
- Enter information using the Family Tree Maker wizard
- Begin your Family File using the Family Page

Starting Family Tree Maker

Before you can enter your family history data into Family Tree Maker, you must be able to launch the program. When Family Tree Maker was installed (see Appendix A, "Installing Family Tree Maker"), the installation set up two different ways for you to launch the Family Tree Maker program.

Launching Family Tree Maker from the Menu

For each program installed on your computer, there is a Start Menu option that allows you to launch the program. Family Tree Maker is no different.

1. **Click** on the **Start button** on the Windows Taskbar. The Start menu will appear.

2. **Move** the **mouse pointer** to Programs. The Programs menu will appear.

3. Move the **mouse pointer** to Family Tree Maker. The Family Tree Maker menu will appear.

4. Click on **Family Tree Maker**. Family Tree Maker will start.

Launching Family Tree Maker from the Desktop

Family Tree Maker installs an icon on the Windows desktop that saves you time and steps by taking you directly to the Family Tree Maker program.

1. Double-click on the **Family Tree Maker icon**. Family Tree Maker will start.

NOTE

The desktop in Windows is the main screen you see when you first boot up your computer. This screen has icons for different programs you have installed, as well as other items that were installed by Windows the first time you turned on the computer.

Creating a New Family File

The first step to using Family Tree Maker is to enter information about your family. For most of us, this means taking the bits and pieces shared by family members and entering them into the program.

Using the Family Tree Maker Wizard

Family Tree Maker offers an easy introduction to help you enter data about yourself and your family. As soon as Family Tree Maker opens, a wizard will appear to help you enter information.

NOTE

Family Tree Maker will prompt you for a file name for your new Family File. After you type a file name in the File name field, just click on the Save button.

1. Type your **name** in the Your name field.

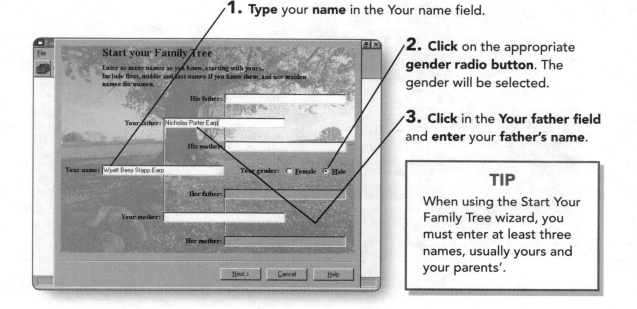

2. Click on the appropriate **gender radio button**. The gender will be selected.

3. Click in the **Your father field** and **enter** your **father's name**.

TIP

When using the Start Your Family Tree wizard, you must enter at least three names, usually yours and your parents'.

NOTE

To find out how to bypass the wizard, please see the next section, "Beginning Directly in the Family Page."

4. Press the **Tab key**. The cursor will move to the Your mother field.

5. Type your **mother's name** in the Your mother field.

6. Press the **Tab key**. The cursor will move to the His father field.

Start your Family Tree

Enter as many names as you know, starting with yours. Include first, middle and last names if you know them, and use maiden names for women.

His father: | Walter Earp
Your father: | Nicholas Porter Earp
His mother: | Martha Ann Early
Your name: | Wyatt Berry Stapp Earp   Your gender: ○ Female ● Male
Her father:
Your mother: | Virginia Ann Cooksey
Her mother:

Next >   Cancel   Help

7. Type the **name** of your father's father in the His father field.

8. Press the **Tab key.** The cursor will move to the His mother field.

9. Type the **name** of your father's mother in the His mother field.

Start your Family Tree

Enter as many names as you know, starting with yours. Include first, middle and last names if you know them, and use maiden names for women.

His father: | Walter Earp
Your father: | Nicholas Porter Earp
His mother: | Martha Ann Early
Your name: | Wyatt Berry Stapp Earp   Your gender: ○ Female ● Male
Her father:
Your mother: | Virginia Ann Cooksey
Her mother:

Next >   Cancel   Help

10. Press the **Tab key**. The cursor will move to the Her father field.

11. Type the **name** of your mother's father in the Her father field.

12. Press the **Tab key.** The cursor will move to the Her mother field.

13. **Type** the **name** of your mother's mother in the Her mother field.

14. **Click** on the **Next button**. The Births screen will appear.

15. In the Date Born field, **enter** the **date of birth** for the first person in the Births window.

16. **Press** the **Tab key**. The cursor will move to the Location field.

17. **Type** the **place of birth** for that person.

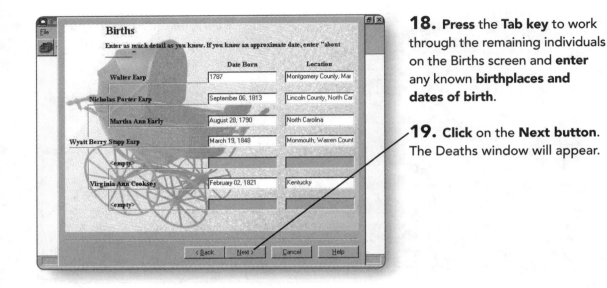

18. Press the **Tab key** to work through the remaining individuals on the Births screen and **enter** any known **birthplaces and dates of birth**.

19. Click on the **Next button**. The Deaths window will appear.

20. In the Date Died field, **type** the **date of death** for the first person in the Deaths window.

21. Press the **Tab key**. The cursor will move to the Location field.

22. Enter the **place of death** for that person.

23. Click on the **Next button** when you have finished entering death information for each person. The FamilyFinder Search window will appear.

24. Click on the **Click here if you don't want to search check box.** The option will be selected.

25. Click on the **Finish button.** A Family Tree Maker message box will appear, telling you that you can run a search any time by clicking on the FamilyFinder icon.

26. Click on **OK**. The message box will disappear.

NOTE

You will be introduced to the FamilyFinder search and report in Chapter 10, "Searching Your Family Tree File."

TIP

If the Cue Card appears, press the Escape key to close it. For more information on the Cue Card, see Chapter 2, "Understanding Family Tree Maker."

Beginning Directly in the Family Page

While the wizard guides you through the initial entry of the basic information about yourself and some immediate family members, you might wish to bypass it and begin entering information directly into the Family Page in Family Tree Maker.

1. Click on the **Cancel button**. A message box will appear, asking you whether you want to go to the Family Page.

2a. Click on **Yes**. The message box will disappear and you will go directly to the Family Page.

OR

2b. Click on **No**. The message box will disappear and you will go back to the wizard.

3. Click on **OK** in the Cue Card. The Cue Card will disappear.

NOTE

See Chapter 3, "Family Tree Maker for Beginners," for information on how to enter information in the empty Family Page.

BUILDING FROM ANOTHER PERSON'S RESEARCH

It is possible that you are not starting from scratch, but instead you are building from the research done by another family member. Most researchers today are using some form of genealogical software. If they are willing to share, you will want to ask them to send you a GEDCOM (GEnealogical Data COMmunication) file. Family Tree Maker can import this file into your Family File. See Chapter 21, "Working with GEDCOM Files and Other Family Files," for more information.

2

Understanding Family Tree Maker

Learning any new program requires an introduction to the program's interface. There are usually some new menu items, push buttons, and choices that are specific to the program. This is true of Family Tree Maker, and this chapter introduces you to those items. In this chapter, you'll learn how to:

- Execute commands using menus and toolbars
- Use dialog boxes and scroll bars
- Navigate the various Family Page fields
- Select different views
- Move information
- Exit Family Tree Maker

Exploring Family Tree Maker

When you look at the Family Tree Maker screen, you will see a number of buttons and tabs. These buttons allow you to perform the different tasks in the program. The tabs allow you to maneuver through your family history database. This section introduces you to these features.

Using Menus

Menus are lists of the functions built into software programs. The Family Tree Maker menus are activated by clicking on the words that appear along the top bar of the Family Tree Maker window. Each menu contains a list of related commands.

1. **Click** on a **menu name**. The menu you chose will appear.

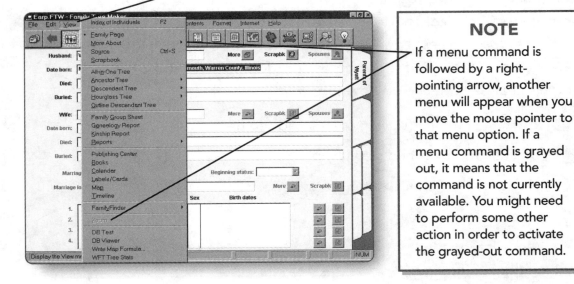

NOTE

If a menu command is followed by a right-pointing arrow, another menu will appear when you move the mouse pointer to that menu option. If a menu command is grayed out, it means that the command is not currently available. You might need to perform some other action in order to activate the grayed-out command.

TIP

Some menu commands have keyboard shortcuts. You will find the keyboard shortcuts listed to the right of the menu command. You can use these shortcuts to execute commands, rather than using the menus. To learn about some of the most popular keyboard shortcuts, see Appendix B, "Using Keyboard Shortcuts."

2. Move the **mouse pointer** over a menu item with a right-pointing arrow. A second menu will appear.

3. Move the **mouse pointer** over an option on the second menu. The menu item will be highlighted.

TIP

Click on a menu option to execute that command. This might change the view of the screen, open a dialog box requesting additional information or choices, or open another window.

Using Toolbars

There is one toolbar in Family Tree Maker. The toolbar offers buttons to access some of the more popular views, as well as a few shortcut buttons to some of the unique commands.

1. Move the **mouse pointer** over each of the toolbar buttons. A tip describing the function of that toolbar button will appear.

2. Click on the **Family Page button** on the toolbar. The Family Page will appear.

NOTE

When you click on the various toolbar buttons or make certain menu choices, Family Tree Maker will open a Cue Card. The Cue Card offers some tips for working with that option.

TIP

If you do not wish to see the Cue Cards, you can turn them off. Click on the Click here if you don't want to see this Help Window again check box, then click on the OK button. To learn more about turning this feature on and off, see Chapter 23, "Working with System Preferences."

Understanding Dialog Boxes

In Family Tree Maker, dialog boxes allow you to make choices and select additional options. They also allow you to select items or preferences. Before you work with the example in this section, be sure you are in the Family Page, which is the default screen in Family Tree Maker, and that you're working with a family that has both a husband and a wife.

1. Click on **People**. The People menu will appear.

2. Click on **Other Spouses**. The Other Spouses dialog box will open.

TIP

You can also access the Other Spouses dialog box by pressing the F3 key.

Moving around with Scroll Bars

In Family Tree Maker, scroll bars are found to the right of and at the bottom of windows, where the text or report extends beyond the limits of the window. There are three different ways to move up and down or sideways using the scroll bars.

1. Click on the **Descendant Tree button**. The Descendant Tree menu will appear.

2. Click on **Fan**. The Descendant Fan Tree window will appear.

- **Click** on the **arrow** at either end of the vertical (or horizontal) scroll bar. This will scroll the page up or down (or side to side) one line at a time.

- **Press and hold** the **mouse button** on the vertical (or horizontal) scroll box and **drag** the **scroll box** up or down (or side to side) within the scroll bar. This allows you to move through more of the page at a time.

- **Click** inside the **vertical (or horizontal) scroll bar**. This moves the page up or down (or side to side) one screen at a time.

Navigating the Fields

When you work in the main entry screens of Family Tree Maker, you will need to jump from field to field to enter the appropriate information. Since much of what is taking place at this time is done on the keyboard, keyboard commands are the easiest way to do this.

1. Click on the **Family Page button**. The Family Page will appear.

2. Navigate through the **fields** using one of the following methods.

- **Press** the **Tab key** to move from one field to another within the Family Page.

- **Press** the **Enter key** to move from one field to another within the Family Page.

- **Press** the **up arrow or down arrow** to move from one field to another within the Family Page.

As you move through the fields, each field that the cursor arrives at will be highlighted.

NOTE

When you navigate in the Family Page using any of the keyboard commands, you will notice that you move from one field to the next where typing is allowed. Family Tree Maker will bypass any other options on the page.

---

3. Type some new **information** in one of the fields. The highlighted field's information will change.

CAUTION

You do not want to use this method to change the order of children. Do not simply highlight the child in question and type the name of the new child. Doing this simply changes the name of the already entered individual; it does not rearrange the children. Methods of rearranging children are examined in Chapter 4, "Enhancing the Family."

Understanding the Different Views

Family Tree Maker offers different views to display the family data. Some of these views are limited to a single-family unit, while others display multi-generational charts of ancestors, descendants, or both.

Exploring the Family Page

The Family Page is where you will spend the most time. This is where you'll enter much of your data and where you'll access the other areas in which data can be entered.

1. Click on the **Family Page button**. The Family Page will appear.

2. Click on the **More button**. The More About window will appear.

3. Click on the **Family Page button**. The Family Page will appear.

4. Click on the **Scrapbk button**. The Individual Scrapbook window will appear.

5. Click on **View**. The View menu will appear.

6. Click on **Family Page**. The Family Page will appear.

7. Click on the **Spouses button**. The Spouses of dialog box will open.

NOTE

You will work more closely with the Spouses of dialog box in Chapter 3, "Family Tree Maker for Beginners."

Looking at the Individual Facts Card

The Individual Facts Card offers you everything you can access through the Family Page buttons in one easy-to-use window, complete with tabs and options.

1. Click on **View**. The View menu will appear.

2. Click on **Individual Facts Card**. The Individual Facts Card will appear.

NOTE

When you are in the Family Page, the only way to access the Individual Facts Card is through the View menu.

NOTE

To learn how to work with the Individual Facts Card, see Chapter 9, "Understanding Individual Facts Cards."

Working with the Ancestor Tree

The Ancestor Tree view offers a chart of the ancestors of a selected individual. There are three different formats in which to display this information.

1. Click on the **Ancestor Tree button**. The Ancestor Tree menu will appear.

2a. Click on **Fan**. The Fan Chart will appear.

OR

2b. Click on **Standard**. The Standard Ancestor Tree will appear.

OR

2c. Click on **Vertical**. The Vertical Ancestor Tree will appear.

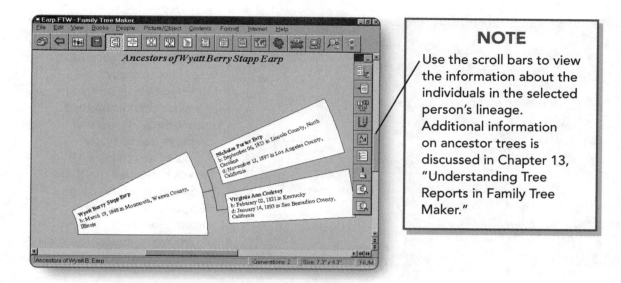

NOTE

Use the scroll bars to view the information about the individuals in the selected person's lineage. Additional information on ancestor trees is discussed in Chapter 13, "Understanding Tree Reports in Family Tree Maker."

Working with the Descendant Tree

The Descendant Tree view offers a chart of the descendants of a selected individual. There are two different formats in which you can display this information.

1. Click on the **Descendant Tree button**. The Descendant Tree menu will appear.

2a. Click on **Fan**. The Fan Chart will appear.

OR

2b. Click on **Standard**. The Standard Descendant Tree will appear.

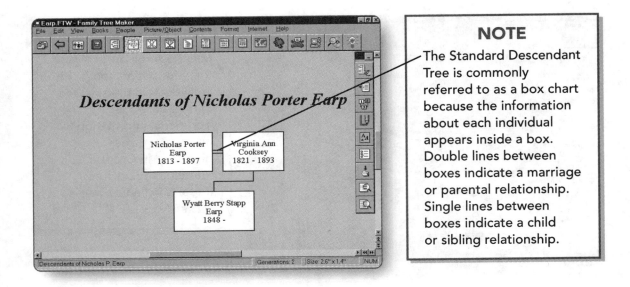

NOTE

The Standard Descendant Tree is commonly referred to as a box chart because the information about each individual appears inside a box. Double lines between boxes indicate a marriage or parental relationship. Single lines between boxes indicate a child or sibling relationship.

Working with the Hourglass Tree

The Hourglass Tree view offers a chart of both the descendants and ancestors of a selected individual. There are two different formats in which you can display this information.

1. **Click** on the **Hourglass Tree button**. The Hourglass Tree menu will appear.

2a. **Click** on **Fan**. The Fan Chart will appear.

OR

2b. **Click** on **Standard**. The Standard Hourglass Tree will appear.

NOTE

The Standard Hourglass Tree also uses the box format to display ancestors and descendants.

Moving Information

Family Tree Maker allows you to use Windows' Copy and Paste functions to move information from field to field.

1. **Place** the **mouse pointer** in front of the first character you want to select and **click and drag** the **pointer** until you reach the last character you wish to cut or copy. The selected text will be highlighted.

2. Click on **Edit**. The Edit menu will appear.

3. Click on either **Cut Text or Copy Text**. The selected text will be placed on the Clipboard.

NOTE

The Cut Text command removes the text from the highlighted field and places it on the clipboard. The Copy Text command leaves the text in the highlighted field and creates a copy on the Clipboard.

4. Click in the **field** where you want to paste the information.

5. Click on **Edit**. The Edit menu will appear.

6. Click on **Paste Text**. The copied (or cut) text will appear in the field you selected.

Exiting Family Tree Maker

You now have seen the basics of the Family Tree Maker program. When you are finished working in the program, you will want to close it.

1. Click on **File**. The File menu will appear.

2. Click on **Exit**. Family Tree Maker will close.

NOTE

You can also close the program by clicking on the Close button (☒) in the upper-right corner of the Family Tree Maker window.

3

Family Tree Maker for Beginners

Most of your time with Family Tree Maker will be spent entering the data you have uncovered about your family. At first, this information will be about yourself, your parents, and perhaps your grandparents. However, eventually you will find yourself with ancestral lines that go back many generations. Family Tree Maker helps you keep that information straight. In this chapter, you'll learn how to:

- Enter a primary individual
- Enter an event
- Change the date format
- Add a spouse
- Add children
- Add an additional spouse
- Move a child to the primary individual position

Entering a Primary Individual

Family Tree Maker allows you to record the information for each individual in your family history. The Family Page lets you enter specific information for the husband, wife, and children.

1. **Type** the **husband's name** in the Husband field.

NOTE

The primary individual can be entered in either the Husband field or the Wife field, depending on his or her gender.

TIP

An individual's name is made up of given names (first and middle names) and the surname (last name), typed in that order.

2. **Press** the **Tab key**. The cursor will move to the Date born field.

NOTE

Notice that when the Tab key is pressed, it bypasses the options to the right of the husband's name. These features are accessed by clicking on them or by pulling down the appropriate menu item.

UNDERSTANDING NAMES IN FAMILY TREE MAKER

Generally, when entering the name of an ancestor in Family Tree Maker, you will simply type the name (as it appears in the record or resource you are viewing) directly into the Name field in Family Tree Maker's Family Page. However, there are a few instances where the surname (last name) is not just a single word. In such instances, it is necessary to identify the surname for Family Tree Maker. This is done by surrounding the surname with backward slashes (\). There are many different reasons why a surname might be more than one word. This is especially true in the research of European names. Here are some examples, with the backward slash included, to give you an idea of what such a name should look like.

George \de la Vergne\

Peter \Van Der Voort\

Pierre \Bourbeau dit Lacourse\

Teresa \Garcia Ramirez\

Another instance in which you might need to use backward slashes is when entering someone who does not have a last name, such as a person of Native American descent. For instance, your ancestor might have been known as Running Bear. This name would be entered in Family Tree Maker as Running Bear\\.

Entering an Event

When you record your family history, you first must concentrate on names, dates, and places. Therefore, Family Tree Maker includes these basic fields in the Family Page.

1. Type a **date** in the Date born field.

2. Press the **Tab key**. The cursor will move to the in field.

TIP

The traditional method for recording dates is to enter the numerals of the day, followed by the first three letters of the month, followed by the full four numerals of the year. Family Tree Maker defaults to a different setting. You'll learn how to change this setting later in this chapter, in the "Changing the Date Format" section.

3. If known, **type** a **birth location** in the in field.

4. Press the **Tab key**. The cursor will move to the Died field.

NOTE

When you enter the place name, use commas to separate the different divisions. Places should always be entered from smallest division, such as a town, to largest division, such as a state or country. Generally the country is omitted when it is the United States.

5. Type a **date** in the Died field, if known.

6. Press the **Tab key**. The cursor will move to the in field.

7. Type a **location** in the in field, if known.

Changing the Date Format

As I mentioned earlier, Family Tree Maker's default for dates does not coincide with the standard followed in the genealogical community. However, this is easy enough to change.

1. Click on **File**. The File menu will appear.

2. Move the **mouse pointer** to Preferences. The Preferences menu will appear.

3. Click on **Dates & Measures**. The Dates & Measures dialog box will open.

NOTE

In the Dates & Measures dialog box, you can set the cutoff date for double dating. Double dating was the result of the change from the Julian to the Gregorian calendar. The Gregorian calendar determined that January would be the first month of the year. This took place for England, one of the last countries to change, and its colonies in 1752.

4. Choose the **DMY option** to conform to standard genealogical dating. The option will be selected.

5. Select the **Month style** from the Styles drop-down menu. The standard method is to use the first three letters of the month.

TIP

Similar drop-down menus are available for changing the separator between the day, month, and year, and also for the format of the names of each day.

6. Click on **OK**. The Dates & Measures dialog box will close.

The selections made in the Dates & Measures dialog box will automatically take effect in the Family Page.

Adding Individuals

Researching family history involves recording names, dates, and places. Programs like Family Tree Maker help make that easier by keeping track of the familial connections as you enter them.

Adding a Spouse

The Family Page is designed to include information about the husband, wife, and children, and it provides you with data fields in which you can type certain basic facts about each one. Now that you have entered the information about the husband, it is time to add the wife.

1. **Type** the **wife's name** in the Wife field and **press** the **Tab key**. The cursor will move to the Date born field.

2. **Enter** the **birth date** and **press** the **Tab key**. The cursor will move to the in field.

3. **Type** the **place of birth** and **press** the **Tab key**. The cursor will move to the Died field.

4. **Enter** the **death date** and **press** the **Tab key**. The cursor will move to the in field.

5. **Type** the **place of death** and **press** the **Tab key**. The cursor will move to the Buried field.

6. **Enter** the **burial date** and **press** the **Tab key**. The cursor will move to the in field.

7. **Type** the **place of burial** and **press** the **Tab key**. The cursor will move to the Marriage date field.

8. **Enter** the **marriage date** and **press** the **Tab key** twice. The cursor will move to the Marriage location field.

TIP

The Beginning status drop-down menu allows you to select the type of relationship between the two individuals. For most of them you will select the Married option. For more on this feature, see Chapter 20, "Working with Marriage Facts and Custom Fact Names."

9. **Type** the **place of marriage** in the Marriage location field.

Adding Children

When you add children in the Family Page, you can enter the basics about each child. You can easily enter each child's full name, gender, and date of birth.

1. **Type** the **name** of the first child in the 1 field and **press** the **Tab key**. The cursor will move to the Sex field.

2. **Enter** the **sex** and **press** the **Tab key**. The cursor will move to the Birth dates field.

3. Type the **date of birth** and **press** the **Tab key**. The cursor will move to the 2 field for the name of the next child.

NOTE

You can add as many children as necessary. When you press the Tab key after each birth date, Family Tree Maker will take you to the next child line, where you can enter the information for the next child. For more on this, see Chapter 4, "Enhancing the Family."

Adding an Additional Spouse

The Family Page only allows one spouse to be displayed at a time. However, there are times when a researcher needs to enter more than one spouse for an individual. Family Tree Maker can support multiple spouses.

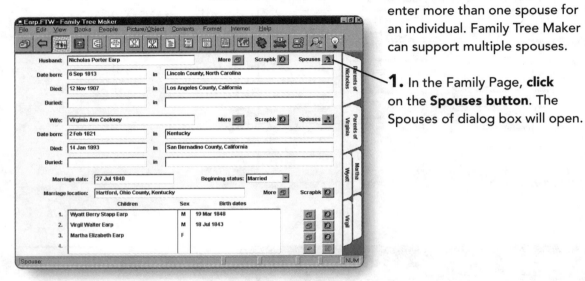

1. In the Family Page, **click** on the **Spouses button**. The Spouses of dialog box will open.

2. Click on the **Create a new spouse button**. A message box will appear, asking if you want the new spouse to be associated with the children previously entered for an individual.

3a. Click on **Yes**. The children will have the new spouse as one of their parents.

OR

3b. Click on **No**. The children will not have the new spouse added as their parent.

4. In the Wife field, **type** the **name** of the new spouse.

5. Enter the **information** you know about the marriage event.

Designating a Preferred Spouse

Family Tree Maker requires that one spouse be selected as the preferred spouse for when you are working with reports and displaying the family in the Family Page.

1. In the Family Page, **click** on the **Spouses button**. The Spouses of dialog box will open.

NOTE

Notice that the Spouses button now displays two small people. This lets you know that the individual has more than one spouse.

2. Click on the **spouse** you want as the preferred spouse. The spouse will be highlighted.

3. Click on the **Make the high-lighted spouse the preferred spouse button.** The preferred spouse character will show at the left of the selected individual.

4. Click on **OK**. The Spouses of dialog box will close.

Switching to Another Spouse

Because you can only view the information and children of one spouse, it is necessary to switch spouses when you want to work on that specific family. You also need to change spouses if you want to add additional information about that particular marriage.

1. Click on the **Spouses button**. The Spouses of dialog box will open.

2. Select the **spouse** for the marriage on which you want to work. The spouse will be highlighted.

3. Click on **OK**. The Spouses of dialog box will close.

NOTE

The Family Page now displays the selected spouse. However, you have not made this spouse the preferred spouse. You can edit information about the spouse or the marriage, or add additional children at this point.

TIP

Family Tree Maker will tell you how many children and spouses are known for the individual highlighted in the Family Page.

Moving a Child to the Primary Individual Position

After you have entered the children, it is possible that you will want to concentrate on a specific child. To do this, you move that child to the primary husband or wife position.

1. Drag the **scroll bar** next to the children information until you find the child with whom you want to work.

NOTE

The names that appear in the tabs at the right of the screen will change as the names in the Children section change.

2. Click on the **tab** for the selected child.

The child will replace the parent in the Husband or Wife field, and all of the other fields on the Family Page will change in accordance with the information currently known about that child.

Part I Review Questions

1. How do you open Family Tree Maker? *See "Starting Family Tree Maker" in Chapter 1*

2. How do you create a new Family File? *See "Creating a New Family File" in Chapter 1*

3. How do you discover the keyboard shortcuts available in Family Tree Maker? *See "Using Menus" in Chapter 2*

4. How are dialog boxes used in Family Tree Maker? *See "Understanding Dialog Boxes" in Chapter 2*

5. What are the three ways to move from one field to another in Family Tree Maker? *See "Navigating the Fields" in Chapter 2*

6. What are some of the main views found in Family Tree Maker? *See "Understanding the Different Views" in Chapter 2*

7. In what view do you enter the name of an ancestor? *See "Entering a Primary Individual" in Chapter 3*

8. How can you change the way dates are displayed in Family Tree Maker? *See "Changing the Date Format" in Chapter 3*

9. Can you have more than one spouse for an individual? *See "Adding an Additional Spouse" in Chapter 3*

10. How do you make the child the primary individual? *See "Moving a Child to the Primary Individual Position" in Chapter 3*

PART II

Using Family Tree Maker Features

4

Enhancing the Family

The family structure in a genealogical search is constantly changing. You are always finding new individuals that need to be connected in your database. In this chapter, you'll learn how to:

- Add parents
- Add siblings
- Line up children
- Add additional parental links

Adding Parents

It is likely that when you were working through Chapter 3, "Family Tree Maker for Beginners," you entered information about your immediate family. Now you want to add the parents of one of those people you entered.

1. Click on the **Family Page button**. The Family Page will appear.

2. Click on the **Parents tab** for either the husband or the wife. A new Family Page with the basic information for one child will be displayed. The child whose basic information is displayed is the individual who was the husband or wife in the previous screen.

3. Enter the **father's name** in the Husband field.

4. Enter the **father's birth and death information** in the appropriate fields.

5. Enter the **mother's name** in the Wife field.

6. Enter the **mother's birth and death information** in the appropriate fields.

TIP

When typing the names of females, you will always enter them with their maiden name. That is the surname they had at birth.

NOTE

There will be times when you do not know the maiden name of the woman. The proper way to enter an unknown surname is to use the following set of characters: [--?--]. However, be aware that Family Tree Maker will question such a surname.

7. Type the **parents' marriage date** in the Marriage date field.

8. Select a **beginning status** from the Beginning status drop-down menu. You will probably choose Married for this option.

9. Enter a **marriage location** in the Marriage location field.

TIP

If you prefer not to use your mouse, press the Tab key after entering the marriage date. This will take you to the Beginning status drop-down menu. You can then change the status by pressing the up or down arrow key. When you have selected the Beginning status you want, press the Tab key to move the cursor to the Marriage location field.

Working with Children

When working in the Family Page, you will find that there are times when you need to add additional siblings. Also, it is through the Children fields that you have the opportunity to add another set of parents in addition to the child's natural, or biological, parents.

Adding Siblings

After you have added the information for the parents, you will want to work on your ancestor's siblings.

1. Click in the **2 field**.

2. Type the **name** of the next known child, as well as the rest of the information known about that child.

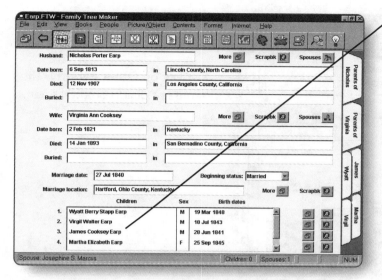

3. Enter the **next child's information** and continue to **add information** for the rest of the children in the family.

NOTE

There will be times when the children you have entered are not in their correct birth order. You will learn how to adjust their order in the "Arranging Child Order" section later in this chapter.

Adding Another Set of Parents

Due to adoption, there will be times when you will have two sets of parents for an individual. Or, in other cases, an individual might have a stepparent. Naturally, you want to record all the information for that person.

1. Click on the **child** you wish to select. The child will be selected.

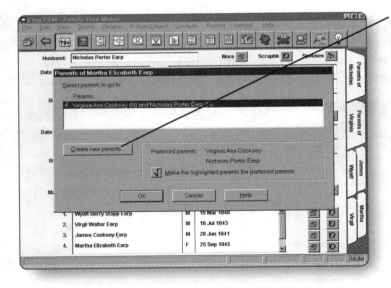

2. Click on **People**. The People menu will appear.

3. Click on **Other Parents**. The Parents of dialog box will open.

4. Click on the **Create new parents button**. The Create New Parents dialog box will open.

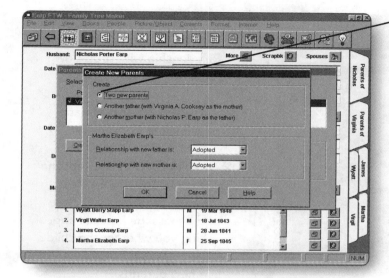

5. Select either **Two new parents, Another father,** or **Another mother.**

NOTE

Notice that when you select Another father or Another mother, the relationship options reflect the selection. You can only change the relationship for the chosen parent.

6. Click on the **Relationship with down arrow**. The Relationship with drop-down menu will appear.

7. Select the appropriate **relationship** from the list.

8. Click on **OK** to accept the selection. The Create New Parents dialog box will close and a message box will appear, asking you whether the child's siblings should be attached to the new parent(s).

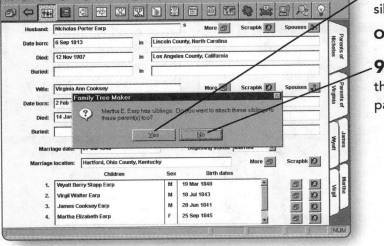

9a. Click on **Yes** to attach the siblings to the new parent(s).

OR

9b. Click on **No** to attach only the selected child to the new parent(s).

10. Type the **parent's name** in the appropriate name field. Notice that the information for the remaining parent has carried over, and that the child's information has been brought to the new screen.

Arranging Child Order

In a perfect world, you would already know everything about all the children in a particular family. However, this is not usually the case. There will be times when you will need to add a child or change the order of the children previously entered.

Adding a Child

The best way to add an additional child to the list of children is to select the Insert Child option.

1. Click on the **Family Page button**. The Family Page will appear.

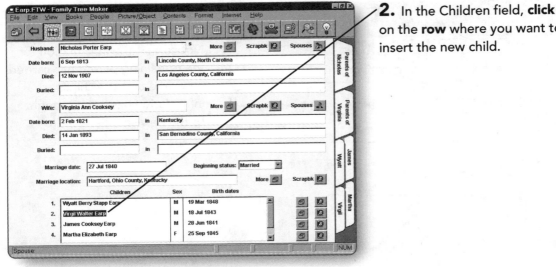

2. In the Children field, **click** on the **row** where you want to insert the new child.

3. Click on **People**. The People menu will appear.

4. Click on **Insert Child**. Family Tree Maker will insert a blank child row.

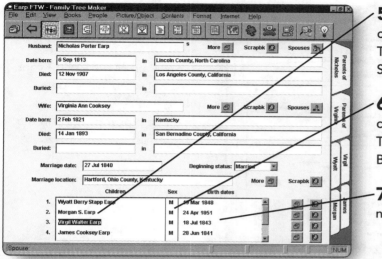

5. Enter the **name** of the new child and **press** the **Tab key**. The cursor will move to the Sex field.

6. Type the **sex** of the new child and **press** the **Tab key**. The cursor will move to the Birth dates field.

7. Enter the **birth date** of the new child.

Moving a Child

After you have entered or updated a child's information, you might need to move the child so that he or she appears in the proper birth order.

1. Select the **child** you wish to move. The child will be selected.

2. Click on **People**. The People menu will appear.

3. Click on **Move Child From**. A message box will appear, telling you how to move the child into a new position in the Children list.

4a. Click on **OK** to continue with the move.

OR

4b. Click on **Cancel** to stop the move.

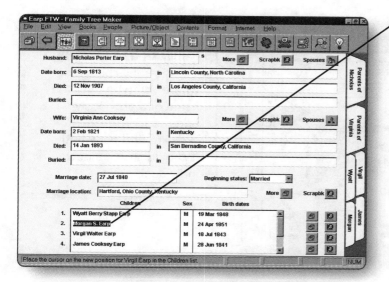

5. In the Children field, **click** on the **position** where you want to move the child.

6. Click on **People**. The People menu will appear.

7. Click on **Move Child To**. The child will move to the new position.

CAUTION

To move a child, you cannot just type over the previously entered child's name. Family Tree Maker uses internal tracking that is not altered when you do this. If there are spouses or descendants associated with the original child, such a manual change could ruin the links previously created.

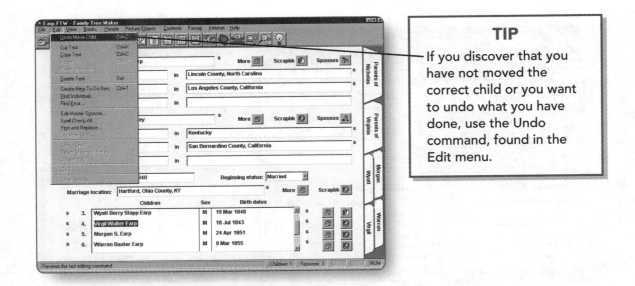

NOTE

Family Tree Maker will question any change where you type over the name of a previously entered individual, in order to find out whether it should create a new individual.

TIP

If you discover that you have not moved the correct child or you want to undo what you have done, use the Undo command, found in the Edit menu.

Sorting Children

If you are working with records that do not list the children in order, it is not necessary to figure out the correct order before entering them on the Family Page. Family Tree Maker offers a Sort command that will rearrange the children chronologically after you have entered them.

1. Click on **People**. The People menu will appear.

2. Click on **Sort Children**. A dialog box will appear, confirming that you want to sort the children by birth order (oldest first).

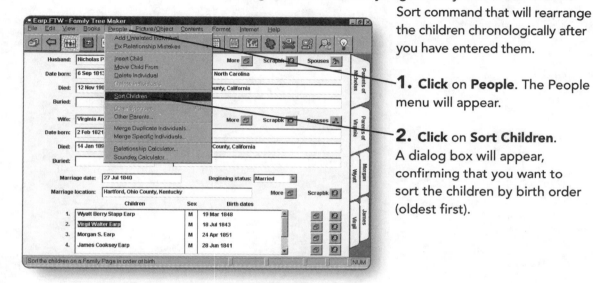

3. Click on **OK** to have Family Tree Maker arrange the children in this order.

5

Documenting Sources

Citing the sources on which you are relying is one of the most important aspects of your research. Citing sources helps you keep track of the records you have used, which helps you avoid wasting time revisiting sources. In this chapter, you'll learn how to:

- Determine where you can cite a source
- Cite a source
- Create a master source
- Change a master source
- Search for a master source

Where Can You Cite Sources?

Family Tree Maker makes it possible for you to cite sources for the names of individuals and each of their specific events. This allows you to document your research so that others with whom you share information will know what you used to draw your conclusions.

1. **Click** on the **Family Page button**. The Family Page will appear.

2. **Click** on **View**. The View Menu will appear.

3. **Click** on **Source**. The Source-Citation dialog box will open.

You can cite sources in several fields, including these:

- Name
- Birth date and location
- Death date and location
- Burial date and location
- Marriage date and location
- Marriage ending date and location
- Each of the Fact fields
- Cause of death
- Medical information

Citing a Source

There are a few steps you need to take to create a source and cite it as proof of an individual event (or of a person's life as a whole). You will first create a master source listing; then, you can select it when you want to cite that source again.

Creating a Master Source

The master source is information about a source that doesn't change. For example, the author, title, and publication information don't change for a book. However, items like the page number from which the information comes will change depending on the person about whom you are entering data.

1. Click on **Edit**. The Edit menu will appear.

2. Click on **Edit Master Sources**. The Master Source dialog box will open.

3. Type the **book title** in the

TIP

You only need to enter a source one time. You can then recall it from the list the next time you want to cite it as proof of an individual's specific event. This is especially useful when a lot of information comes from a single source, such as a book. Remember that for every event or conclusion you include in your Family File, you should have a source cited.

Title of source field and **press the Tab key**. The rest of the fields will be activated and the cursor will move to the Author/Originator field.

NOTE

The Title of source field has been programmed so that the title will print out in italics when source citations are included on reports.

4. Enter the **author's name** and **press** the **Tab key**. The cursor will move to the Publication facts field.

5. Type the **publication information**.

6. Select the **type of media** from the Source media drop-down menu.

7. Type the **call number** in the Call number field and **press** the **Tab key**. The cursor will move to the Source location field.

NOTE

The call number is the number assigned to the source in the repository where it was found. This could be a microfilm number, a Dewey Decimal system number, or some other numbering system unique to that particular library or archive.

8. Enter the **source location** and **press** the **Tab key**. The cursor will move to the Comments field.

NOTE

The source location might be a library, archive, county courthouse, or cousin's residence. The source location is where the original source used exists. You want to know this so that if you need to refer back to it, you know exactly where to return.

9. Type your **comments** and **press** the **Tab key**. The cursor will move to the Source quality field.

NOTE

The Comments section offers you a place to put your thoughts about the source and the information included in that source. This information is not included when the source is printed on reports; it is only for your personal reference.

10. Enter the **quality** of the source.

NOTE

The quality of the source is your reference to how reliable the source is. If the source is difficult to read because of unclear handwriting or faded ink, then it is possible that the information found could be questioned.

11. Click on **OK**. The Master Source dialog box will close.

Using the Source-Citation Dialog Box

The Source-Citation dialog box is where you will select the appropriate master source for the information you are citing.

You can enter source information when you enter the data and details for each ancestor.

1. Click in the **field** where you want to add a source citation.

2. Click on **View**. The View menu will appear.

3. Click on **Source**. The Source-Citation dialog box will open.

TIP

You can also use the keyboard shortcut Ctrl+S to launch the Source-Citation dialog box. Whether you access it this way or through the menu, the source citation will be attached to the highlighted field or the last field in which you were working.

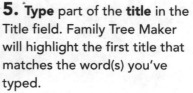

4. Click on the **Find Master Source button**. The Find Master Source dialog box will open.

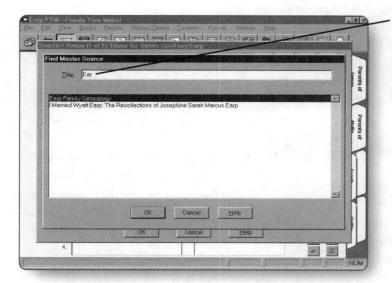

5. Type part of the **title** in the Title field. Family Tree Maker will highlight the first title that matches the word(s) you've typed.

TIP

If you have a lengthy list of sources, you can use the scroll bar to quickly scroll through the list.

6. Click on the desired **source** in the list. The source will be selected.

7. Click on **OK**. The Find Master Source dialog box will close.

NOTE

Notice that the title of the source and the printed format of the footnote are now displayed in the Source-Citation dialog box.

8. Type the **page number** of the citation in the Citation Page field.

NOTE

Not all source citations will have a page number included on this screen. For more information about source citations, read Elizabeth Shown Mills's *Evidence! Citation and Analysis for the Family Historian* (Genealogical Publication Co., 1997).

9. Enter the **Citation text** in the Citation Text field. The citation text might be further identifying information. For instance, when citing a census record, you would want to include the Enumeration District, Supervisor's District, Dwelling number, and Family number for the specific house of your ancestor on that census page.

TIP

You can decide whether to include text from the Citation Text field in the printed footnote. Click on the Include citation text in footnote check box if you want the text to be included. If the text is just for your information, make sure the box is not checked.

10. Click on **OK** to close the Source-Citation dialog box.

Notice that there is now an "s" next to the field where you elected to cite the source. This is how you know that you have cited a source for either an individual or an event.

Creating a Master Source from the Source-Citation Dialog Box

Few of us are so organized that we already know all of the sources that we will be citing before we begin. While you're working on a family, you might find that an obscure source was not added to the master source list earlier. You do not need to exit out of the Source-Citation dialog box to add a master source.

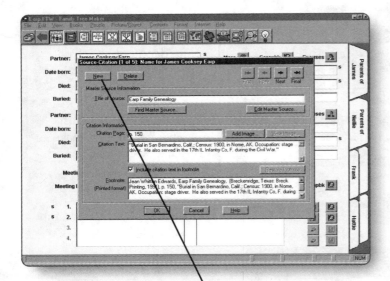

1. Press Ctrl+S to open the Source-Citation dialog box.

NOTE

It is possible that the Source-Citation dialog box already has a previously cited source. You can have more than one source citation per person or event.

---

2. Click on the **New button**. Family Tree Maker will start a new source citation, and the cursor will move to the Title of source field.

3. Type the **title** of the new source. The Edit Master Source button will be activated.

4. Click on the **Edit Master Source button**. The Master Source dialog box will open.

TIP

Notice that the Title of source field has been disabled in the Master Source dialog box. You cannot change the title at this time. For more information on editing master sources, see the "Changing a Master Source" section later in this chapter.

5. Enter the **appropriate source information**.

6. Click on **OK**. The Master Source dialog box will close.

You can now complete the source citation with the page number and citation text as you learned in the "Using the Source-Citation Dialog Box" section earlier in this chapter.

7. **Click** on **OK**. The Source-Citation dialog box will close.

Changing a Master Source

While we would all like to think we are perfect, there will be times when you will discover that you've made an error. In a source, that should be fixed as soon as it is noticed. Usually you will notice such an error when you're working with that source in the Source-Citation dialog box.

1. **Click** on **View**. The View menu will appear.

2. **Click** on **Source**. The Source-Citation dialog box will open.

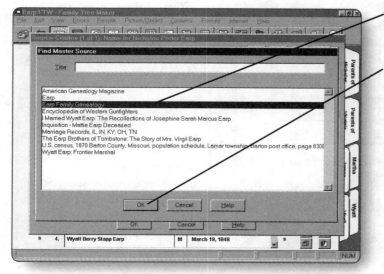

3. Click on the **Find Master Source button**. The Find Master Source dialog box will open.

4. Select a **master source** from the list of available sources.

5. Click on **OK**. The Find Master Source dialog box will close. You will notice that the Edit Master Source button has now been activated in the Source-Citation dialog box.

6. Click on the **Edit Master Source button**. The Master Source dialog box will open.

7. Make the appropriate **changes** to the master source fields. Usually you'll be changing a typo or fixing the publication date.

NOTE

The Title of source field is grayed out when you access the master source in this manner. To edit the title of a master source, see "Editing a Master Source" in the next section.

---

8. Click on **OK**. The Master Source dialog box will close.

NOTE

Notice that the changes you made to the source have taken effect in the printed format of the footnote.

Editing a Master Source

While accessing the master source through the Source-Citation dialog box is easy, you cannot change the title of the source this way. If you have a lot of editing to do to a master source, you might want to go directly to the master source.

1. Click on **Edit**. The Edit menu will appear.

2. Click on **Edit Master Sources**. The Master Source dialog box will open.

NOTE

You can use the Next, Prev, First, and Final buttons to skip through previously entered master sources. Click on the New button to create a new master source, and use the Delete button to delete the currently displayed master source.

TIP

If you inadvertently type over the name of a source in the Source-Citation dialog box, Family Tree Maker will ask you whether you want to change the present title or create a new source.

Searching for a Master Source

There will be times when you will want to look at a specific master source. The easiest way to do this is through the Master Source dialog box.

1. Click on **Edit**. The Edit menu will appear.

2. Click on **Edit Master Sources**. The Master Source dialog box will open.

3. Click on the **Find Master Source button**. The Find Master Source dialog box will open.

4. **Type** the **first few letters** of the title of the source. The first title containing those letters will be highlighted.

5. **Click** on the **title** of the desired source. The source will be selected.

6. **Click** on **OK**. The Find Master Source dialog box will close.

The selected source will now be in the Master Source dialog box, where you can view it or make changes, if necessary.

Attaching Images to Sources

Modern technology affords us the opportunity to scan documents or microfilm to digitize documents. Family Tree Maker offers you the ability to attach such an image to the Master Source or the specific Source-Citation dialog box.

1. Press Ctrl+S. The Source-Citation dialog box will open.

2. Click on the **Add Image button**. The Get Image From dialog box will open.

3. Select the appropriate **source** of the picture. The option will be selected.

4. Click on **OK**. Family Tree Maker will open a window or launch the appropriate program.

NOTE

For more on working with images in Family Tree Maker, see Chapter 17, "Creating a Scrapbook."

6

Understanding More About Options

Family history is much more than just names and dates of birth or death. As you research further into your family's generations, you will be keeping track of additional events and wanting to add family stories. In this chapter, you'll learn how to:

- Add and work with additional facts
- Add addresses for living relatives
- Track medical information
- Work with the More About Lineage window

Working with the More About Facts Window

Family Tree Maker offers you a way to track additional life events. As your research progresses, you will find that you are relying on such things as probate records and church records, in addition to the more recognizable vital records. Family Tree Maker has included a variety of predefined facts (Family Tree Maker's name for the events in a person's life) to help you record this information.

1. Click on the **Family Page button**. The Family Page will appear.

2. Click on the **More button**. The More About window will appear.

3. Click on the **Facts button**. The More About Facts window will appear.

TIP

You can also access the More About options from the View menu.

Adding Additional Facts

You will record much of the information about your ancestors in the More About Facts window. This is where you will record the variety of life events that you discover.

1. Click on the **Fact down arrow**. The Fact drop-down menu will appear.

2. Click on a **fact** in the menu. The fact will be selected and the menu will close.

3. Press the **Tab key** to advance to the Date field.

NOTE

Many of the facts in the Fact drop-down menu are pertinent to specific religions. This allows you to select the appropriate religious event, rather than making do with, say, a general christening event.

4. Type the **date** of the event and **press** the **Tab key**. The cursor will move to the Comment/Location field.

TIP

Information entered using the More About options can also be added using the Individual Facts Card. For more on this option, see Chapter 9, "Understanding Individual Facts Cards."

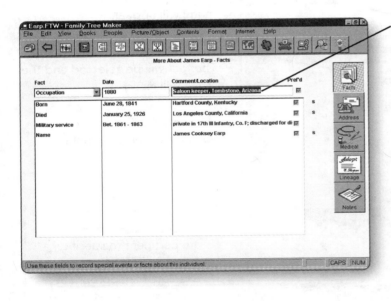

5. Enter the **event location** and **press** the **Tab key**. The new fact will be added, in alphabetical order, to the list of facts for that individual, for those events with full dates.

NOTE

The Pref'd check box is disabled for event-type facts unless you have conflicting or duplicated facts. If you had two death dates, you would select one of them as your preferred choice.

Adding Additional Names

You might discover that your ancestor had another name. It might have been a religious name or a nickname, or it might just be a variant of his or her given name. Family Tree Maker allows you to keep track of these different names. Whereas the AKA (also known as) name option allows you to record one additional name, through the name options here you can record variant name spellings and other names you simply want to remember.

1. **Click** on the **Fact down arrow**. The Fact drop-down menu will appear.

2. **Select** the **Name fact** and **press** the **Tab key**. The cursor will move to the Comment/Location field.

3. **Enter** the **individual's name**.

4a. **Click** on the **Pref'd check box** if you want this name to be the one used in the Family Page and on reports.

OR

4b. **Leave** the **Pref'd check box** empty if you do not want this name to be used in the Family Page and on reports.

Selecting a Preferred Name

Even if you checked the Pref'd check box when you entered a name, you can always change that. For example, when sending reports to a cousin, you might want to use one name; when sharing with your brother or sister, you might want to use another name.

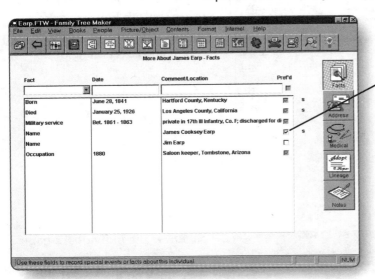

1. Click in the **Pref'd check box** next to the name you want to select. The name will be selected.

2. Click in the **Pref'd check box** next to another name fact. Notice that, in addition to displaying the check mark, the preferred name will appear at the top of the list of name facts.

Creating a New Fact Name

Family Tree Maker includes 41 different facts, but you might need to record an event that is not covered by any of them. You can create a new fact name whenever you need one.

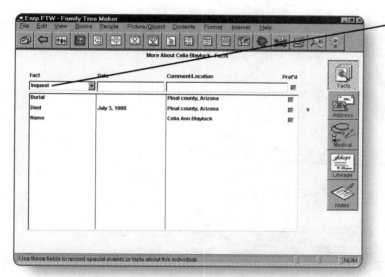

1. **Click** in the **Fact field**.

2. **Type** the **name** of the new event and **press** the **Tab key**. The cursor will move to the Date field.

3. **Enter** the **date** and **press** the **Tab key**. The cursor will move to the Comment/Location field.

4. Type the **event location** and **press** the **Tab key**. Family Tree Maker will open a New Fact Name message box, verifying that you want to accept the new fact name.

5a. Click on **OK** to accept the new fact name. The new fact name will be saved.

OR

5b. Click on **Cancel** to return to the Fact field to type in a different name or select a different predefined fact.

NOTE

You can always get rid of a fact name that you have created. For more information on this, see Chapter 20, "Working with Marriage Facts and Custom Fact Names."

Using the Address Window

The Address window is useful when you're entering data about your living relatives. People involved with a family association rely heavily on this for mailing lists, as do those who want to keep track of cousins with whom they are exchanging information.

1. Click on the **Address button**. The More About Address and Phone(s) window will appear.

NOTE

Notice that the individual's name has already been supplied. Family Tree Maker assumes you are entering the address for the individual currently in the More About window.

2. Type the **street address** in the Street 1 field and **press** the **Tab key** twice. The cursor will move to the City field.

3. Type the **city name** and **press** the **Tab key**. The cursor will move to the State or province field.

4. Type the **state or province** and **press** the **Tab key**. The cursor will move to the Zip or postal code field.

5. Enter the **zip or postal code** and **press** the **Tab key**. The cursor will move to the Country field.

6. Type the **country name** and **press** the **Tab key**. The cursor will move to the Phone(s) field.

7. Enter the **phone number** and **press** the **Tab key**. The cursor will move to the Email(s) field.

8. Enter the **e-mail address**.

TIP

Just because there are fields for all this information does not mean you need to supply it. You need only put in what is important for you to be able to contact the individual at a later date.

Working with Medical Information

Modern medical technology has made understanding your medical family tree more important than ever before. Family Tree Maker provides you with space for recording pertinent medical information about your family members and ancestors.

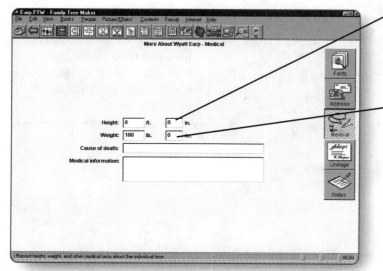

1. Click on the **Medical button**. The More About Medical window will appear.

2. Type the **height** in feet and inches in the Height field and **press** the **Tab key**. The cursor will move to the Weight field.

3. Enter the **weight** in pounds and ounces and **press** the **Tab key**. The cursor will move to the Cause of death field.

4. Type the **cause of death** and **press** the **Tab key**. The cursor will move to the Medical information field.

NOTE

The cause of death will generally be the medical term found on the death certificate, or the illness or condition that caused the individual to die.

5. Enter the **details** you feel are important about your ancestor's medical history.

NOTE

The Medical information field can hold up to 200 characters of information, which is about five lines of text.

Opening the More About Lineage Window

Family Tree Maker uses the More About Lineage window to organize information about relationships, titles, and aliases.

1. Click on the **Lineage button**. The More About Lineage window will appear.

2. Enter any appropriate **information** or **select** one of the available **options**. The next sections will describe some of the different options available in this window.

TIP

When entering a title, do not enter items such as Jr or III. The titles entered here will be printed in front of the individual's name on reports. If your ancestor was a Jr. or a Sr., this is typed into the Name field on the Family Page, at the end of the name and following a comma. When you are indexing your book, the comma becomes necessary in order to distinguish Jr. from the surname. Roman numerals such as III or IV are automatically recognized by Family Tree Maker, so no comma is necessary.

Entering AKA Names

There will be times when you will discover a name change or an alternate name for your ancestor or family member. Legal name changes are just one way the AKA field can be used.

1. Click in the **This person is also known as (aka) field** and **type** the **also known as name** for your ancestor.

TIP

When you print reports, you can elect to use the also known as name instead of or in addition to the name used in the Family Page. Such decisions are made when you are working in the report. For more on this topic, see Chapter 16, "Creating Genealogy Style and Genealogical Source Reports."

Working with Special Relationships

As you dig deeper into your family history, you are apt to discover mothers who died early, fathers who remarried, adoptions, and other unique relationship situations. It is natural to want to record these in Family Tree Maker.

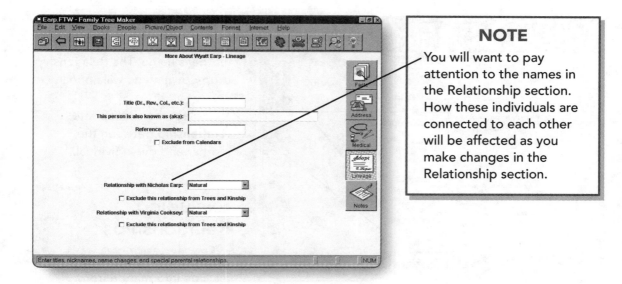

NOTE

You will want to pay attention to the names in the Relationship section. How these individuals are connected to each other will be affected as you make changes in the Relationship section.

1. **Click** on the **Relationship with down arrow** next to the father's name. The Relationship drop-down menu will appear.

2. **Select** the appropriate **relationship** between the father and the individual.

NOTE

You will only be able to select Natural from the drop-down menu for one father and one mother, regardless of how many parents you have added to a person.

3. Click on the **Relationship with down arrow** next to the mother's name. The Relationship drop-down menu will appear.

4. Select the appropriate **relationship** between the mother and the individual.

Excluding Relationships

At times you might want to exclude information from reports you send to family members, possibly out of respect for their feelings. Some of those exclusions are set up in the More About Lineage window.

1. Click on the **Exclude this relationship from Trees and Kinship check box** for either the mother or the father of the individual. The option will be selected and that relationship will be excluded from your reports.

NOTE

Electing to exclude the relationship from Trees and Kinship will affect reports. Kinship reports and Ancestor Trees will exclude the paternal and/or maternal ancestors, depending on which relationship(s) you chose to exclude. Descendant Trees will exclude the child and the child's descendants.

7

Understanding More About Notes

One way to make your family history interesting to other family members is to include family stories. With Family Tree Maker you can do just that. In this chapter, you'll learn how to:

- Enter notes and stories
- Copy and move notes and stories
- Find text in notes
- Import notes
- Export notes
- Format notes for printing

Working with Notes and Stories

Most of us have heard our grandparents, aunts, or uncles share stories about family members. As your research progresses, you will find additional stories. Family Tree Maker's More About Notes window allows you to incorporate these notes and stories into your research.

Entering Notes and Stories

The More About Notes window allows you to enter, in a narrative style, the stories or research notes you want to include in your reports.

1. Click on **View**. The View menu will appear.

2. Move the **mouse pointer** to More About. The More About menu will appear.

3. Click on **Notes**. The More About Notes window will appear.

4. In the text box, **enter** the **text** you wish to include for the individual.

NOTE

The information typed into the Notes window will not print on the family tree styled reports. However, you can print this information on a family group sheet report or include it in a book.

TIP

When quoting information from a source, be sure to include the source citation information. Always put quotation marks around any information that is a direct quote from a published source.

Copying Notes and Stories

Sometimes a particular note might apply to more than one individual. When you are working with such a story, you will want to take advantage of the copy and paste functions available in Family Tree Maker.

1. Click on **View**. The View menu will appear.

2. Click on **Individual Facts Card**. The Individual Facts Card will appear.

3. Click on **Notes**. The Notes tab will appear.

TIP

This is another method of getting to the Notes window for a particular individual.

4. Click and drag the **mouse pointer** to highlight the desired text. The text will be selected.

5. Right-click on the selected **text**. The right mouse menu will appear.

6. Click on **Copy**. The selected text will be placed on the Clipboard, ready for you to paste wherever you like. Chapter 10, "Searching Your Family Tree File," explains how to locate someone in your database who is not included in the current Family Page. You can use these functions to locate an individual to whose Notes window you want to paste the copied text.

TIP

The menu that appears when you right-click is a shortcut menu that allows you to cut, copy, paste, or delete selected text. This is the same as clicking on the Edit menu and selecting the options there.

Moving Notes and Stories

You might discover that a story you thought pertained to one individual was really about another. The easiest way to fix this is to move the story from one More About Notes window to another.

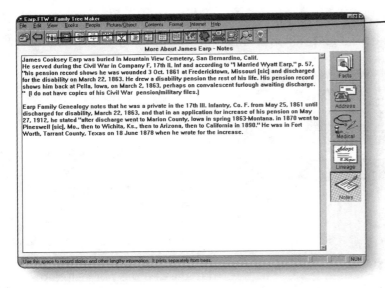

1. Click on the **Family Page button**. The Family Page will appear.

2. Click on the **More button**. The More About window will appear.

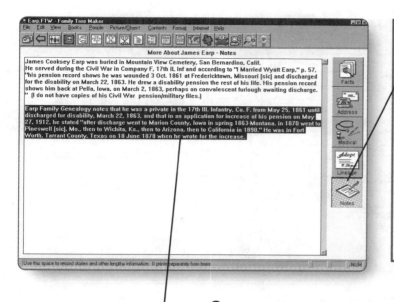

3. Click and drag the **mouse pointer** to highlight the selected text.

4. Click on **Edit**. The Edit menu will appear.

5. Click on **Cut Text**. The selected text will be removed from the More About Notes window and placed on the Clipboard, ready to be pasted in another individual's More About Notes window.

6. Click on the **Family Page button**. The Family Page will appear.

7. Click on the **Name tab** of the individual you want to select. The Family Page will change to reflect the selected individual.

8. Click on the **More button**. The More About window will open. The More About Notes window should be displayed because it was the last More About window used.

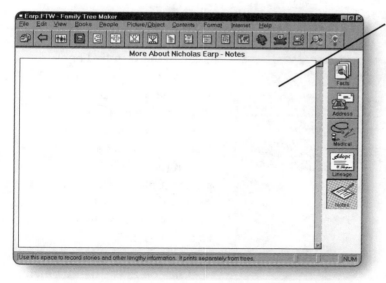

9. **Click** inside the **text box**.

10. **Click** on **Edit**. The Edit menu will appear.

11. **Click** on **Paste Text**. The text will appear in the More About Notes window.

TIP

The keyboard shortcuts Ctrl+X for Cut, Ctrl+C for Copy, and Ctrl+V for Paste can be used instead of the menus.

Finding Text in Notes

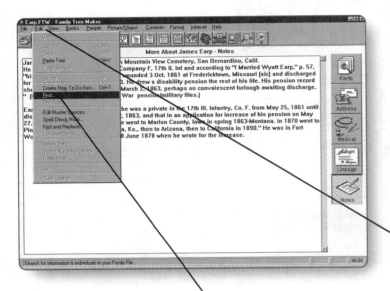

It can be hard to find one particular sentence or thought when you have typed a large amount of text in the More About Notes window. Family Tree Maker offers a way to search for a specific word or phrase. Before you follow these directions, be sure the More About Notes window you want to search is open.

1. Click on **Edit**. The Edit menu will appear.

2. Click on **Find**. The Find dialog box will open.

3. Type the **word or phrase** for which you want to search in the Find what field.

4. Click on the **Find next button**. When Family Tree Maker finds the requested word or phrase, it will highlight it in the More About Notes window.

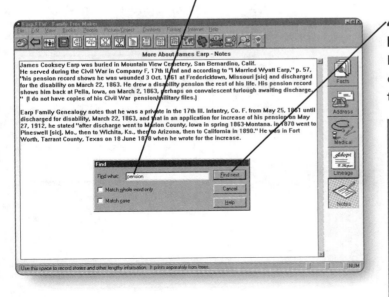

TIP

Family Tree Maker allows you to match whole words or match case. This allows you to eliminate those words that share consecutive letters with the word for which you are looking.

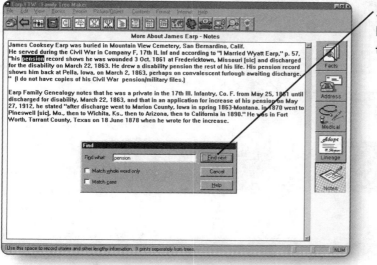

NOTE

If the cursor was not at the beginning of the text in the More About Notes window, then Family Tree Maker might ask you if you want to continue searching from the beginning. Click on Yes if you want to continue searching.

5. Click on the **Find next button** to continue searching the text.

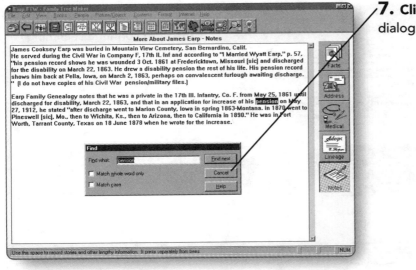

6. Click on **OK** when you see the message box telling you that Family Tree Maker has reached the end of the text. The message box will close and you will be returned to the Find dialog box.

7. Click on **Cancel**. The Find dialog box will close.

Importing Text to Notes

At some point, you might want to import some text into Family Tree Maker. You might have received a write-up via e-mail, or you might have already typed up a family story that you now want to place in the More About Notes window. You can do so by importing the text or by copying and pasting.

Copying Text

The Windows operating system allows you to copy text from one application and paste it into another. Because Family Tree Maker is a Windows program, this option is available to you.

1. **Highlight** the **text** you want to copy from the e-mail message or word-processing file.

2. **Press Ctrl+C** to copy the text. The text will be placed on the Clipboard.

3. **Click** on **Family Tree Maker** in the Windows Taskbar. Family Tree Maker will be maximized.

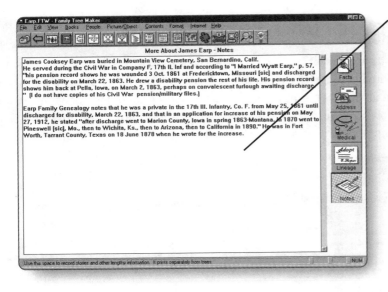

4. Click in the **More About Notes window**, at the location where you want the text to appear. The cursor will appear.

5. Press Ctrl+V. The copied text will appear in the More About Notes window.

Importing Text

Family Tree Maker also allows you to import text. This can be done only when the file you want to import ends in a .txt extension, because that is the only file type that Family Tree Maker recognizes. You need to have the cursor in the More About Notes window where you want the text to appear before you follow these steps.

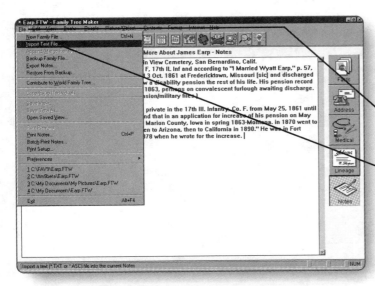

1. Click on **File**. The File menu will appear.

2. Click on **Import Text File**. The Import Text File dialog box will open.

3. Click on the **Look in down arrow.** The Look in drop-down menu will appear.

4. Navigate to the **folder** where the text file is located.

5. Click on the **selected file.**

6. Click on **Open.** The text will be placed in the More About Notes window.

Exporting Notes

You might have notes that you have received from others, and in turn, you might want to share your notes with a cousin or fellow researcher. You can do so by exporting the notes.

1. Click on **File**. The File menu will appear.

2. Click on **Export Notes**. The Export Notes dialog box will open.

3. In the File name field, **type** the **name** of the file you want to export. You will want to pay attention to where the file is being saved so you can retrieve it later.

NOTE

Family Tree Maker will automatically assign the .txt extension to the file name.

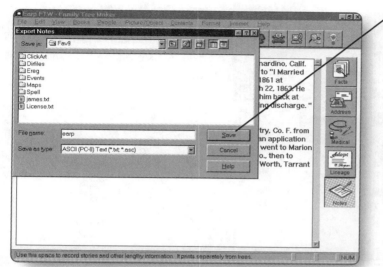

4. Click on **Save**. The text in the More About Notes window will be saved to the file.

Formatting Notes for Printing

With the More About Notes window open, you can format the text's chosen font, style, and size to alter how it appears when printed in the reports. This will make the notes stand out in your report.

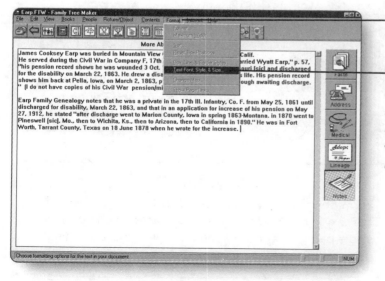

1. Click on **Format**. The Format menu will appear.

2. Click on **Text Font, Style, & Size**. A message box will appear, reminding you that the changes made will display only when you print the report, not on the screen.

3. Click on **OK**. The message box will close and the Text Font, Style, & Size dialog box will open.

4. Select the desired **font** from the Font drop-down menu.

5. Click on **OK**. The Text Font, Style, & Size dialog box will close.

NOTE

The formatting options, which are also used in the reports, are discussed in more detail in Chapter 15, "Viewing and Printing Reports and Trees."

CAUTION

Formatting in the More About Notes window affects all the text in the Notes window. You cannot highlight a single paragraph and change the style on just that single paragraph.

8

Working with More About Marriage

Much of what you have learned up to this point dealt with a specific individual in your database. However, the marriage event is unique, and Family Tree Maker understands that there are different ways to handle it. In this chapter, you'll learn how to:

- Select an ending status for the marriage
- Work with reference numbers
- Select the appropriate marriage fact
- Select a preferred date
- Work with the Marriage Notes window

Accessing the More About Marriage Window

The More About Marriage window allows you to include notes or pertinent additional dates about the marriage of two individuals. While the marriage date itself can be entered on the Family Page, the additional notes and details are entered on the More About Marriage window.

1. Click on the **Family Page button**. The Family Page will appear.

2. Click on the **Marriage More button**. The More About Marriage window will appear.

3. Click on the **Facts button**. The More About Marriage Facts window will appear.

Using the More About Marriage Facts Window

The More About Marriage Facts window is where you can include additional details about a marriage. This is where you would include a divorce fact or a conflicting marriage fact.

1. Click on the **Ending status down arrow.** The Ending status drop-down menu will appear.

2. Select the appropriate **ending status** from the menu.

NOTE

If you don't know how the marriage ended, you can select Unknown from the drop-down menu.

Entering a Reference Number

The Reference number field allows you to enter any numbers or letters you choose. If you have a unique filing or pedigree system, you might use this field for that system's reference number.

1a. Type a **reference number** in the Reference number field.

OR

1b. Leave this **field** blank if you do not have a reference numbering system.

Adding a Marriage Fact

Although you have already entered one marriage fact, there are others that you might need to enter—possibly a conflicting marriage date or a fact that details the end of that marriage.

1. Click on the **Fact down arrow**. The Fact drop-down menu will appear.

2. Click on the **appropriate fact** from the menu and **press** the **Tab key**. The fact will be selected and the cursor will move to the Date field.

TIP

If you select something like the annulment, divorce, or death of one spouse, be sure to change the Ending status to correspond with the fact.

3. Enter the **date** of the event and **press** the **Tab key**. The cursor will move to the Comment/Location field.

4. Type the **location** of the event.

TIP

The small trashcan that shows up when you type a previously-entered place allows you to "trash" what Family Tree Maker is suggesting. If the place is the one you want, you can press the Tab key to accept it and add the fact to the Facts list.

NOTE

There is a connection between the facts in the More About Marriage page and the marriage fact itself. To learn more about this and how it might pertain to unique situations in your research, see Chapter 20, "Working with Marriage Facts and Custom Facts Names."

Using the Pref'd Check Box

The Pref'd check box is activated when you have selected a duplicate fact. This happens when you have two conflicting dates recorded.

1. Select a **duplicate fact** from the Fact drop-down menu.

2. Type the **date** of the event in the Date field and **press** the **Tab key**. The cursor will move to the Comment/Location field.

3. Type the **location** of the event and **press** the **Tab key**. The new fact will appear in the Fact list.

NOTE

Notice that at this point the Pref'd check box is automatically selected. The newly added fact does not become the preferred fact. This means it will not be the marriage fact that appears in any reports you print.

4. Click on the **Pref'd check box** for the second duplicated fact. The newly selected preferred fact will move to the top of the duplicated events and will have a check in the Pref'd check box.

Working with Marriage Notes

Just as you might include stories about an individual as a note, you might also want to record something about a marriage. As it does for individuals, Family Tree Maker supplies you with a More About Notes window for marriages.

1. **Click** on the **Notes button**. The More About Marriage Notes window will appear.

2. **Type** the **text** you want to include about the marriage.

3. Click on **Format**. The Format menu will appear.

4. Click on **Text Font, Style, & Size**. The Text Font, Style, & Size dialog box will open, so you can format your newly added note.

NOTE

Family Tree Maker will remind you that the changes you make to font, style, and size will appear only in your printed reports. Also, remember that these changes will affect the entire note, not just a section of it. Click on OK to close the message box.

NOTE

See Chapter 7, "Understanding More About Notes," to refresh your memory about changing the text in the More About Notes window.

9

Understanding Individual Facts Cards

With the More About button on the Family Page, you have the ability to enter a lot of different information about a person. Sometimes you want easy access to that information. The Individual Facts Card gives you instant access. In this chapter, you'll learn how to:

- Access the Individual Facts Card
- Establish the Individual Facts Card as a default for editing information
- Add a fact
- Add a note
- Switch to another related individual within the Individual Facts Card
- Add a new related individual to the Family File
- Go to the Family Page

Accessing the Individual Facts Card

The Individual Facts Card was designed to offer you instant access to the information and facts for an individual. You can access this card either through a menu option or through one of the reports.

Opening an Individual Facts Card

Regardless of the view you are using in Family Tree Maker, you can always get to the Individual Facts Card for the primary individual by using the menu option.

1. Click on **View**. The View menu will appear.

2. Click on **Individual Facts Card**. The Individual Facts Card will appear.

NOTE

If you are in the Family Page, the View menu is the only way to open the Individual Facts Card.

Accessing the Individual Facts Card from Another View

While you are working in one of the Report views, you might notice that a fact isn't right or that you have a typo in a note. Using the Individual Facts Card, you can immediately correct the problem and then return to the Report view.

1. **Click** on a **report button**. The chosen Report view will appear.

2. **Double-click** on the desired **individual**. The Individual Facts Card for that person will open.

The Individual Facts Card Versus the Family Page

Family Tree Maker allows you to choose between the Individual Facts Card or the Family Page when working in other views. In other words, when you double-click on a person in a Report view, you can either be taken to that person's Individual Facts Card or to the Family Page for that person.

Determining Your Preference

You must first decide which you would prefer to open when working in other views.

1. Click on a **report button**. The chosen Report view will appear.

2. Double-click on the desired **individual**. The Individual Facts Card for that person will open.

When you have the Individual Facts Card selected as your default, you can make any changes to the individual and then click on OK to return to the Report view.

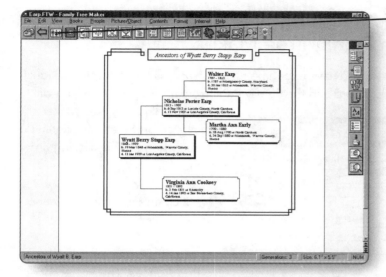

When you access the Family Page from a Report view, it is similar to clicking on the Family Page button on the toolbar. The Family Page will replace the Report view, and you can work in the More About window or the Family Page from there.

TIP

If you are in the Family Page, you can return to the Report view by clicking on the Go Back button.

Establishing Your Preference in Family Tree Maker

Once you have experimented with accessing both the Individual Facts Card and the Family Page from any Report view, you will want to tell Family Tree Maker which you prefer as your default choice when double-clicking on an individual.

1. Click on **File**. The File menu will appear.

2. Move the **mouse pointer** to Preferences. The Preferences menu will appear.

3. Click on **Individual Facts Card**. The Individual Facts Card preferences dialog box will open.

4a. Click on **Individual Facts Card**. The Individual Facts Card option will be selected.

OR

4b. Click on **Family Page**. The Family Page option will be selected.

5. Click on **OK**. The Individual Facts Card preferences dialog box will close and the default will be set.

Working with the Individual Facts Card

The Individual Facts Card dialog box offers you instant access to everything currently known about a given individual. You also have the ability to change or add information, and to select or add another related individual.

Adding a Fact

Through the Individual Facts Card, you have the ability to add just as many facts as you do using the More About window.

1. Click on **View**. The View menu will appear

2. Click on **Individual Facts Card**. The Individual Facts Card will open.

NOTE

If you do not see the Fact, Date, and Comment Location fields above the list of facts for the given individual, you might need to change the display settings in Windows. When Large Fonts has been selected in the display settings, it sometimes forces the list of facts to sit on top of these three fields, which makes it look like they do not work or exist.

3. Click on the **Fact down arrow**. The Fact drop-down menu will appear.

4. Click on the **appropriate fact**. The fact will be selected and the list will disappear.

5. Press the **Tab key**. The cursor will move to the Date field.

6. Type the **date** and **press** the **Tab key**. The cursor will move to the Comment/Location field.

7. Type the **event location**.

8. Click on the **Add button**. The new fact will be added to the individual's list of facts.

TIP

Just like in the More About Facts window (see Chapter 6, "Understanding More About Options"), you can create new facts in the Individual Facts Card. Simply type the name of the new fact and press the Tab key. You can then follow steps 6 through 8 in this section.

Adding a Note

The tabs of the Individual Facts Card mirror the options found in the More About window, accessed from the Family Page. As such, anything that you can add in the More About windows can be added in the Individual Facts Card.

1. Click on the **Notes tab**. The tab will move to the front.

2. Type the **note**.

NOTE

You can access any of the other options, such as the Marriage, Address, or Medical sections, by clicking on the appropriate tab. This brings that section of the Individual Facts Card to the front so that you can work with it. All of these sections mirror their More About equivalents.

Switching to Another Related Individual

While the main menu items are disabled when the Individual Facts Card is open, this does not mean you cannot move to other related individuals. You can change the focus of the Individual Facts card by using the drop-down menus at the bottom of the card.

1. Click on one of the **down arrow choices**. The list of appropriate individuals will appear.

2. Click on the desired **individual**.

The individual will be selected and the Individual Facts Card will pertain to the newly selected individual.

Adding a New Related Individual

When you are entering information about an ancestor, you will often find that the record or book that has supplied you with that information will also supply you with the name or details of a previously unknown, related individual. You can add this person using the Individual Facts Card.

1. Click on the appropriate **down arrow**. The corresponding list will appear.

2. Click on the **Add a menu option**. The menu will disappear and the Individual Facts Card will be blank.

3. Type the **details** for the new person.

Closing the Individual Facts Card

When you are finished making changes or additions to the individual, you can close the Individual Facts Card. Depending on your choice, you will either be returned to the Report view or taken to the Family Page.

1a. Click on **OK**. The Individual Facts Card will close and you will be returned to the Report view.

OR

1b. Click on the **Family Page button**. The Individual Facts Card will close and you will be taken to the Family Page.

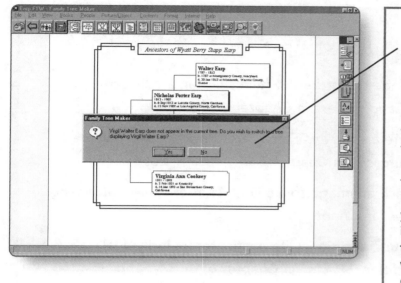

NOTE

If you select another individual or add a new individual and then click on OK, Family Tree Maker might ask you if you want to pull up a new tree with that individual included. Click on Yes to redesign the report, or click on No to revert back to your original report. The information entered in the Individual Facts Card will not be lost if you choose No.

Part II Review Questions

1. How can you change the order in which children are listed?
   See "Arranging Child Order" in Chapter 4

2. Where can you cite a source in Family Tree Maker? *See "Where Can You Cite Sources?" in Chapter 5*

3. How can you attach an image to a source citation? *See "Attaching Images to Sources" in Chapter 5*

4. How can you include additional life events for an individual? *See "Adding Additional Facts" in Chapter 6*

5. How can you copy and paste text in the Notes window? *See "Moving Notes and Stories" in Chapter 7*

6. Can you alter the form and style of notes for printing on reports? *See "Formatting Notes for Printing" in Chapter 7*

7. How do you access the More About Marriage window? *See "Accessing the More About Marriage Window" in Chapter 8*

8. Can you include more than just the marriage event in the More About Marriage Facts window? *See "Using the More About Marriage Facts Window" in Chapter 8*

9. What are the two ways to open an Individual Facts Card? *See "Accessing the Individual Facts Cards" in Chapter 9*

10. Is it possible to add a new related individual to the Family File through the Individual Facts Card? *See "Adding a New Related Individual" in Chapter 9*

Working in Family Tree Maker

10

Searching Your Family Tree File

When you first begin entering data, it is easy to use the tabs along the right side of the window to select the individual you want. However, after you have been researching for a while, you will discover that you have too many people in your files to do this effectively. In this chapter, you'll learn how to:

- Locate individuals using Quick Search
- Work with the Find feature
- Rearrange the index
- Search by name
- Search by other types of criteria
- Work in the FamilyFinder Center

Using Quick Search by Name

The Index of Individuals has a built-in quick search where you can easily type in the name of the individual for whom you are searching. This is the easiest way to locate an individual in your Family Tree file.

1. Click on **View**. The View menu will appear.

2. Click on **Index of Individuals**. The Index of Individuals dialog box will open.

TIP

There are two other ways to access the Index of Individuals dialog box. You can press the F2 key or click on the Index of Individuals button.

3. Click in the **Name field** and **type** the **surname** (last name) of the person you want to find. Family Tree Maker will move the highlight bar to different possible matches as you type.

NOTE

Notice that the highlight bar locates and moves to the first name that fits the letters you have entered. It is usually not necessary to type in the complete surname.

TIP

The Quick Search is not case sensitive. You can type the name in upper-case, lowercase, or mixed case.

Working with the Find Feature

There is a Find feature built into the Index of Individuals dialog box. This is an alternative for those times when the Quick Search is not available.

1. Press the **F2 key**. The Index of Individuals dialog box will open.

2. Click on the **Find button**. The Find Name dialog box will open.

TIP

To find out more about when Quick Search does not work, see the "Rearranging the Index" section later in this chapter.

3. In the Name field, **type** the **name** of the individual you want to find.

4. Click on **OK**. The Find Name dialog box will close and Family Tree Maker will highlight the first individual who fits your search.

TIP

You do not need to type the entire name. You can type just the surname or the first name, and Family Tree Maker will go to the first individual with that name.

5. Click on **Next**. Family Tree Maker will highlight the next individual who fits your search.

TIP

You can also click on the Previous button, and Family Tree Maker will highlight the previous individual who fit your search.

6. Click on the **Go to Family Page button**. The Index of Individuals dialog box will close and Family Tree Maker will display the Family Page for that individual.

TIP

Another way to go to the individual is to click on the OK button. This opens the last window in which you worked for that particular person.

Rearranging the Index

The default arrangement of the Index of Individuals is alphabetical by last name in ascending order. However, you might want to view the list in a different format.

1. Click on **View**. The View menu will appear.

2. Click on **Index of Individuals**. The Index of Individuals dialog box will open.

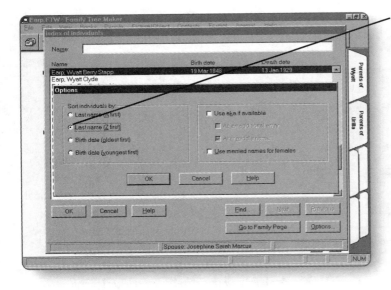

3. Click on **Options**. The Options dialog box will open.

4. Select a different **radio button** in the Sort individuals by list. This will change the order of the Index of Individuals.

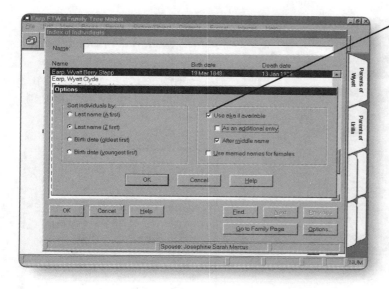

5. Click on the **Use aka if available check box** if you want the also known as name to display in the Index of Individuals.

6. Click on the **As an additional entry check box.** Family Tree Maker will create a new entry in the Index using the nickname.

7. Click on the **After middle name check box.** Family Tree Maker will add the nickname to the original Index entry, placing it after the individual's middle name.

8. Click on the **Use married names for females check box**. Family Tree Maker will change the surname for each female in the index to display her married surname.

NOTE

Selecting the married names changes the surnames of all the females in the list so that they are listed by their married names instead of their maiden names, but it offers an easy way to list females for whom you don't have a maiden name.

9a. Click on **OK**. The Options dialog box will close and your changes will take effect.

OR

9b. Click on **Cancel**. The Options dialog box will close, but the changes will not take effect.

NOTE

If you have changed the Sort individuals by option to something other than Last name (A first), the Quick Search Name field will be disabled.

Using the Find Individual Feature

While you will often search for an individual by name or by scrolling through the Index of Individuals, Family Tree Maker understands that you might also need to look for individuals in a different manner. You can do this using the Find Individual feature.

1. Click on the **Family Page button**. The Family Page will appear.

NOTE

The Find Individual menu option is available only when you are in the Family Page.

2. Click on **Edit**. The Edit menu will appear.

3. Click on **Find Individual**. The Find Individual dialog box will open.

Searching by Name

Of course, you can still use the Find Individual feature to search for individuals by name.

1. Type the **name** for which you want to search in the for field.

NOTE

The Find Individual dialog box defaults to a name search.

2. Click on the **Find next button**. Family Tree Maker will locate the first individual in the database with the name for which you are searching.

3. Click on the **Find next button** again. Family Tree Maker will display the next individual in the database with the name for which you are searching.

TIP

If you accidentally pass the individual you wanted, click on the Find previous button to go back in the search.

NOTE

You can recreate the same search by clicking on the Restart search button.

Searching by Date

At some point, you might want to determine who in your database was born or married prior to a specific date. The Find Individual feature has the ability to search for dates.

1. Click on the **Search down arrow**. The Search drop-down menu will appear.

2. Click on the **Birth date option** and **press** the **Tab key**. The option will be selected and the cursor will move to the for field.

TIP

To select other Search fields, use the scroll bar in the Search drop-down menu.

3. Type the **date** in the for field.

4. Click on the **Find next button**. Family Tree Maker will display the first Family Page with a date that fits the search criteria.

TIP

Continue to click on the Find next button until you find the individual in whom you are interested.

5. Click on **Cancel**. The Find Individual dialog box will close.

Searching by Location

After names and dates, the item in which researchers are most interested is location. The Find Individual feature allows you to search for a specific location.

1. Click on the **Search down arrow**. The Search drop-down menu will appear.

2. Click on the **Birth location option** and **press** the **Tab key**. The option will be selected and the cursor will move to the for field.

3. Type the **location** in the for field.

TIP

Family Tree Maker will recall the place as you begin to type. If the place in question is the one you want, you do not need to type the whole name.

4. Click on the **Find next button**. Family Tree Maker will display the More About Facts screen for the first individual who fits the search criteria.

5. Continue to click on the **Find next button** until you find the individual in whom you are interested.

6. Click on **Cancel**. The Find Individual dialog box will close, and the More About Facts window for the last individual found will be displayed.

Searching by Source

You can also use the Find Individual feature to search for a specific source or to determine for which events and individuals you have cited a source.

1. Click on the **Search down arrow**. The Search drop-down menu will appear.

2. Click on the **Birth source info option** and **press** the **Tab key**. The option will be selected and the cursor will move to the for field.

TIP

Selecting Any and all text fields is a quick way to look through all text fields for a word.

3. Type the **word** for which you are looking in the for field.

4. Click on the **Find next button**. Family Tree Maker will display the first individual's record that contains the word for which you are searching.

TIP

To see the text in question, you must open the More About window and look through the text fields.

Searching by Comment

You might be interested in discovering for which individuals you have entered medical information or other comments. You can do this using the Find Individual feature.

1. **Click** on the **Search down arrow**. The Search drop-down menu will appear.

2. **Click** on one of the **comment fields** in the menu and **press** the **Tab key**. The comment field you chose will appear in the Search field and the cursor will move to the for field.

3. **Enter** the **word** for which you want to search.

4. **Click** on the **Find next button**. Family Tree Maker will display the More About screen for the first person who fits the search criteria.

TIP

To find comments with any text, replace the word with != and Family Tree Maker will show you everyone who has any text in that comment field.

Working with the FamilyFinder Center

The FamilyFinder Center offers a number of different methods for searching and researching. At this point, I will concentrate on how to use the FamilyFinder Search and view the generated report.

1. Click on the **FamilyFinder Center button**. The FamilyFinder Center will open.

2. Click on **Run a FamilyFinder Search**. A message box will appear, asking you whether you want to create a FamilyFinder Report.

3a. **Click** on **OK**. The message box will close and the Create New FamilyFinder Report dialog box will open.

OR

3b. **Click** on **Cancel**. A blank FamilyFinder Report will be displayed.

4. **Select** either **Online or CD FamilyFinder Index** in the Search section.

5. **Select** either **All individuals or Selected individuals** in the Include section.

6. **Click** on **OK**. Your browser will launch if you selected the Online option, which is the most thorough. When the search is complete, a message box will appear, telling you how many matches were found.

NOTE

If you click on the Individuals to Include button, the Individuals to Include dialog box will open. You might want to use this option when you have added some new individuals but you do not want the report to be rerun for everyone in the Family File.

FamilyFinder search results are ranked by stars.

Family Tree Maker's new more precise searching means that a 5-star rank is a near-certain match!

If you get any 5-star matches, they display in their own section at the top of your FamilyFinder Report, with an explanation of how many names that source should add to your tree.

★ ★ ★ ★ ★

Getting new Family Archive matches...
You can continue to use your web browser.

19%

Cancel

NOTE

See Chapter 14, "Working with Reports," and Chapter 22, "Working with Custom Reports and Research Journal Features," for more information on working with the FamilyFinder Center.

Search Results:

The FamilyFinder Search found 1243 new matches, the best of which is ranked 5-star.

5 stars mean a virtually positive match!

OK

Select Edit:Create New FamilyFinder Report to create this report.

7. Click on **OK**. The FamilyFinder Report will be displayed.

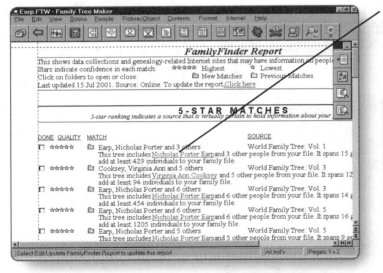

8. Click on the **file folder** for one of your matches. The FamilyFinder Report will give you more details about the match.

9. Double-click on the **ancestor's name**. The Individual Facts Card for that individual will appear.

TIP

The more stars next to an entry, the higher the probability of the match being your ancestor.

NOTE

A star will appear on the Family Page next to anyone with a match in the FamilyFinder report.

11

Correcting Information in Family Tree Maker

In a perfect world, each piece of information you placed in your Family Tree file would be accurate and you would never need to make any changes. However, since no one is infallible when entering data, Family Tree Maker offers ways to undo family relationships, check your spelling, and delete individuals. In this chapter, you'll learn how to:

- Use the spelling checker
- Undo a marriage
- Delete individuals from your Family File
- Check for data entry errors

Working with the Family Tree Maker Spelling Checker

While we'd all like to think we don't make mistakes, there are times when, in typing the details of a will or the place of birth based on a faded record, you might not always get the spelling correct. However, you might not notice the error right away.

Checking Spelling in the Entry Screens

You can ask Family Tree Maker to spell check all the notes and text items in a book from the entry screens and report windows.

1. **Click** on **Edit**. The Edit menu will appear.

2. **Click** on **Spell Check All**. The Spell Check dialog box will open and Family Tree Maker will move to the first Notes screen and highlight the first word not found in the dictionary.

NOTE

It is important to understand that the spelling checker is going to go through all of your Notes screens when it is launched in this manner.

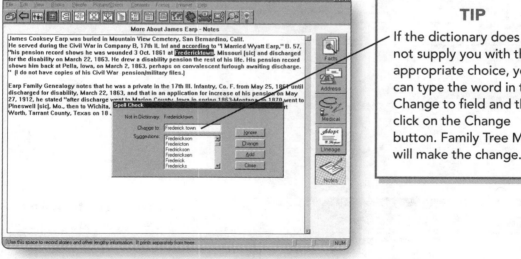

3a. **Click** on **Ignore** to ignore the word and move on in the spell check.

OR

3b. **Click** on **Change** to replace the highlighted word with the word listed in the Change to field.

OR

3c. **Click** on **Add** to place the highlighted word in the dictionary.

TIP

If the dictionary does not supply you with the appropriate choice, you can type the word in the Change to field and then click on the Change button. Family Tree Maker will make the change.

NOTE

When the spelling checker highlights a word, it does not necessarily mean that the word is misspelled. It simply means that the word is not yet in the spelling checker's dictionary.

Checking Spelling in the Notes Windows

When you have finished entering the details in a More About Note or a More About Marriage Note, you might want to make a habit of running the spelling checker while you have the Notes window open.

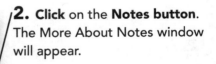

1. In the Family Page, **click** on the **More button**. The More About window will appear.

2. Click on the **Notes button**. The More About Notes window will appear.

3. Click on **Edit**. The Edit menu will appear.

4. Click on **Spell Check Note**. The spelling checker will start.

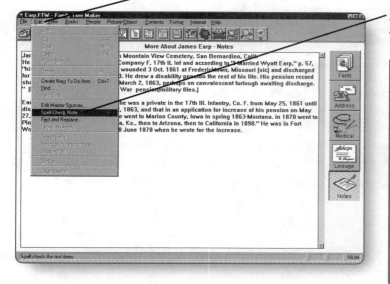

NOTE

When the spelling checker is finished with that specific note, it will ask whether you want to check the other notes in the Family File. Clicking on Yes will run the spelling checker on all the other notes in the family file. Clicking on No will end the spelling check.

Untying the Marriage Knot

As you continue with your research, you might discover that your information about a marriage is inaccurate. This is especially likely when you get into areas where you have multiple generations of the same name (for instance, John Smith, son of John Smith). Family Tree Maker includes options for undoing a marriage if you discover that the individuals you listed as married are not the correct two people.

1. Click on the **Family Page button**. The Family Page will appear.

2. **Click** on the **Index of Individuals button**. The Index of Individuals dialog box will open.

3. **Type** the **name** of the individual for whom you need to untie a marriage.

4. **Click** on the correct **individual** in the list, if he or she is not already selected.

5. **Click** on **Go to Family Page**. The Family Page for the selected individual will appear.

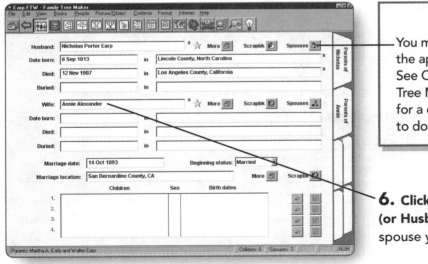

NOTE

You might need to select the appropriate spouse. See Chapter 3, "Family Tree Maker for Beginners," for a quick review on how to do this.

6. **Click** in the **Wife (or Husband) field** for the spouse you want to detach.

7. Click on **People**. The People menu will appear.

8. Move the **mouse pointer** to Fix Relationship Mistakes. The Fix Relationship Mistakes menu will appear.

9. Click on **Detach Spouse**. Family Tree Maker will open a message box, verifying that you want to detach the spouse.

10. Click on **OK** to confirm the change.

NOTE
Any children associated with the marriage will remain with the spouse who was not detached.

Removing People from Your Files

Detaching a spouse removes the individual from the marriage, but it does not remove the individual from your Family File. However, you might discover that you have an individual or group that needs to be deleted completely from the database.

Deleting One Person

When you discover a single individual who should be removed from the database, you can delete that person in the Family Page.

1. Click on the **Family Page button**. The Family Page will appear.

> **TIP**
>
> The individual you want to delete must be listed in the Family Page. Use the Index of Individuals or Find Individual options, if necessary, to select the person you want to delete.

2. Click in the **name field** for the individual you want to delete.

3. Click on **People**. The People menu will appear.

4. Click on **Delete Individual**. A message box will appear, verifying that you want to delete the individual.

5a. Click on **Yes** if you want to delete the individual.

OR

5b. Click on **No** if you do not want to delete the individual.

Deleting a Group of People

If you want to delete a group of individuals, you can select them via the Tree views and the Custom Report. The group of individuals to be deleted must be visible on the report in order for you to delete them as a group.

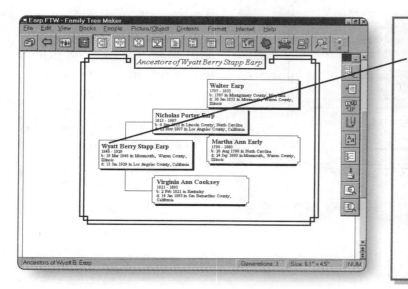

1. Click on a **Tree button**. The selected Tree menu will appear.

2. Click on a **Tree style**. The appropriate Tree window will appear.

TIP

You can use the Custom Report to select those individuals who are not necessarily related by blood or descent.

NOTE

Look at the primary person on the report. It is important to verify that the primary person and those related to that person and displayed on the report are indeed the individuals you wish to delete. If the person isn't the individual you want, you can use the Index of Individuals to select a new person.

3. Click on the **Index of Individuals button**. The Index of Individuals dialog box will open.

4. Type the **name** of the desired individual in the Name field.

5. Click on the correct **individual** in the list, if he or she is not already selected.

6. Click on **OK**. The Index of Individuals dialog box will close and the newly selected individual will be displayed in the report.

7. Click on **People**. The People menu will appear.

8. Click on **Delete Individuals in Ancestor Tree**. A message box will appear, verifying that you do indeed want to delete the individuals from your Family File. The actual wording of this menu item will differ, depending on the type of report or Tree you selected.

9a. **Click** on **Yes**. The individuals will be deleted from the Family File.

OR

9b. **Click** on **No**. The individuals will not be deleted from the Family File.

Checking the Family File for Errors

Family Tree Maker offers you three different ways to scan your Family File for errors. One is automatic, another runs a scan when you request it, and the third is a report of the errors that Family Tree Maker has found.

Data Entry Checking

Family Tree Maker offers a feature that works automatically after it is turned on. This data entry checking feature will let you know when you have entered a questionable date or a name error.

1. Click on **File**. The File menu will appear.

2. Move the **mouse pointer** to Preferences. The Preferences menu will appear.

3. Click on **Error Checking**. The Error Checking dialog box will open.

4. Click on the **Name errors check box**. Family Tree Maker will check for name errors.

5. Click on the **Unlikely birth, death, and marriage dates check box**. Family Tree Maker will check for date errors.

6. Click on **OK**. The Error Checking dialog box will close.

NOTE

When you type in a date that doesn't coincide with the other dates for an individual or family, Family Tree Maker will open a Data Entry Error message box to point out the problem.

Using the Find Error Command

The Find Error command is like a spelling checker for the dates that have been entered. It identifies the errors and then allows you to fix or skip each error.

1. Click on the **Family Page button**. The Family Page will appear.

2. Click on **Edit**. The Edit menu will appear.

3. Click on **Find Error**. The Find Error dialog box will open.

4. Select the **errors** for which you want to search. You can search for name errors and/or unlikely birth, death, and marriage dates by selecting the appropriate check box(es).

5. Click on **OK**. Family Tree Maker will search your Family File for errors. When an error is found, you will have several options.

NOTE

The Reset all ignored errors button allows you to overwrite the Ignore error check box you will be introduced to in the next set of steps.

6a. **Click** on the **Find next button**. Family Tree Maker will bypass the error and find the next one.

OR

6b. **Click** on the **AutoFix button**. Family Tree Maker will change the error based on where it thinks the information should be placed.

OR

6c. **Click** on the **Ignore error check box**. Family Tree Maker will ignore the error now (and in the future, if you want it to).

NOTE

If you turn on the Ignore error check box, Family Tree Maker will ignore the error each time you run Find Error until you click on the Reset all ignored errors button at the start of the Find Error search. The Ignore error check box can be used to have Family Tree Maker bypass those idiosyncrasies unique to the names or dates you are entering.

TIP

If you selected AutoFix in error, or if the change made by Family Tree Maker is not correct, click on Undo. If you use the Undo feature, you will not move to the next error until you click on the Find next button.

Working with the Data Errors Report

From time to time it is a good idea to run the Data Errors Report. This lists all the potential errors that Family Tree Maker identifies in your Family File. After printing this report, you can take time to read through it and determine what in your Family File you might need to change.

1. Click on **View**. The View menu will appear.

2. Move the **mouse pointer** to Reports. The Reports submenu will appear.

3. Click on **Data Errors**. The Data Errors Report window will appear.

4. Click on an **individual** to highlight that person in the list. Notice the potential error.

5. Double-click on the **individual** to edit his or her information. The Individual Facts Card for that individual will appear.

6. Correct the **error** in the Individual Facts Card.

7. Click on **OK** to return to the Data Errors Report to work on the next error. The Data Errors Report will reappear.

12

Fixing Relationships and Duplicates

Sometimes after you have imported a cousin's GEDCOM or data from World Family Tree, you will discover that you have some duplicate individuals. At other times, you might find that you need to adjust the relationship between a child and the parents. In this chapter, you'll learn how to:

- Link children to their parents
- Detach a child from the wrong parents
- Link individuals by marriage
- Merge duplicates
- Search and replace

Fixing Relationships

There will be times when it will be necessary to change the relationships between the individuals in your Family File. Family Tree Maker recognizes that, as your research progresses, there will be times when you will discover an error in how you have connected individuals in a family structure.

Linking Children to Their Parents

You might discover that you already have a child and his or her parents entered in your Family File, but you did not realize they were related when you added them. It's easy to link children to parents in Family Tree Maker.

1. Click on the **Family Page button**. The Family Page will appear.

2. Click on the **Index of Individuals button**. The Index of Individuals dialog box will open.

TIP

You can also access the Index of Individuals dialog box by pressing F2.

3. Click on the **individual** you want to include on the Family Page.

4. Click on **OK**. The Family Page will show the new individual.

NOTE

You need to select one of the parents of the child you wish to add.

5. Click on **People**. The People menu will appear.

6. Move the **mouse pointer** to Fix Relationship Mistakes. The Fix Relationship Mistakes menu will appear.

7. Click on **Attach Child**. The Select the Child dialog box will open.

8. Type the **name** of the individual you want to add as a child.

9. Click on the **name** of the individual in the list.

10. Click on **OK**. A message box will appear, verifying that you want to attach the individual as a child on the Family Page.

11a. Click on **Yes**. The child will be added to the Family Page.

OR

11b. Click on **No**. The child will not be added to the Family Page.

NOTE

If the child in question has siblings from another relationship, Family Tree Maker will ask whether the siblings should also be associated with the new parents.

Detaching a Child from the Wrong Parents

If you discover that a child has been linked to the wrong parents, you can easily detach the child from that family. This will not delete the child from the Family File.

1. Press F2. The Index of Individuals dialog box will open.

2. Type the **name** of one of the parents in the Name field.

3. Click on the correct **name** in the list.

4. Click on **OK**. The family will be displayed in the Family Page.

5. Click on the **child** you want to detach in the Children list.

6. Click on **People**. The People menu will appear.

7. Move the **mouse pointer** to Fix Relationship Mistakes. The Fix Relationship Mistakes menu will appear.

8. Click on **Detach Child**. A message box will appear, asking whether you want to detach the individual's siblings from the parents too.

9a. Click on **Yes**. The siblings of the child will also be detached.

OR

9b. Click on **No**. The siblings of the child will not be detached.

Linking Individuals by Marriage

Unlike typing the names of two spouses in the Family Page, the steps for linking two previously entered individuals require picking one of the individuals out of a list.

1. Click on **View**. The View menu will appear.

2. Click on **Index of Individuals**. The Index of Individuals dialog box will open.

3. Click on the **individual** you want as one of the spouses.

4. Click on **Go to Family Page**. The Family Page will appear.

NOTE

There must be a place for the spouse to go. This means that in the Family Page, the spouse field must be empty. If the individual in question already has a spouse, you need to use the Spouses button to add the spouse. See Chapter 3, "Family Tree Maker for Beginners," for a quick review of how to do that.

5. Click on **People**. The People menu will appear.

6. Move the **mouse pointer** to Fix Relationship Mistakes. The Fix Relationship Mistakes menu will appear.

7. Click on **Attach Spouse**. The Select the spouse dialog box will open.

8. Click on the **name** of the individual you want to select as the spouse.

9. Click on **OK**. A message box will appear, asking whether you're sure you want to make the selected individual the spouse.

10a. Click on **Yes**. The spouse will be attached.

OR

10b. Click on **No**. The spouse will not be attached.

Fixing Duplicates

Often, when you are adding information from a fellow researcher, you will end up with duplicate individuals in your Family File. Sometimes the duplication is the result of entering an individual twice.

Fixing Duplicate Files for the Same Person

Family Tree Maker offers a method to merge individuals that looks not only at the name of the individuals, but also at additional information, such as family relationships.

1. Click on the **Family Page button**. The Family Page will appear.

2. Click on **People**. The People menu will appear.

3. Click on **Merge Duplicate Individuals**. A message box will appear, reminding you to back up your file before you merge duplicate individuals.

4. Click on **OK**. The Merge Duplicate Individuals dialog box will open.

5. Click on **Display merge report**. The Merge Individuals Report window will appear.

NOTE

If Family Tree Maker cannot find duplicates, a message box will appear, telling you that none were found.

TIP

You can click on an individual in the list to get some additional information about the differences between the two possible duplicates.

6. Click on **Done**. The Merge Duplicate Individuals dialog box will reappear.

7. Click on **Merge matching information**. The Merge Individuals dialog box will open.

NOTE

Family Tree Maker automatically merges two individuals with the same information. You are given the option of whether to merge two individuals with differing information.

8a. Click on **Merge**. The two individuals will be merged.

OR

8b. Click on **Don't merge**. The two individuals will not be merged.

NOTE

After you have merged individuals, Family Tree Maker will remind you that you can undo the merge, provided that you do it before you exit the program. Click on OK to close the message box, and then print out and read through the Merge Report to make sure everything was merged correctly.

TIP

In addition to viewing the Merge Report, be sure to view the individuals in the various views to verify that everything is correct. If it's not, you can use the Undo option to undo the merge. You must do this before exiting Family Tree Maker.

Merging Specific Individuals

There are times when you will want total control over the individuals you wish to select for merging. You gain this control using the Merge Specific Individuals menu option.

1. Press F2. The Index of Individuals dialog box will open.

2. Select one **individual** you wish to merge.

3. Click on **OK**. The Family Page will open.

4. Click on **People**. The People menu will appear.

5. Click on **Merge Specific Individuals**. The Select the individual who is the same as dialog box will open.

6. **Enter** the **name** of the second individual in the Name field.

7. **Click** on the **name** of the person with whom you wish to merge the first individual.

8. **Click** on **OK**. A message box will appear, verifying that the individuals should be merged.

9a. **Click** on **Yes**. The two individuals will be merged and the Merge Individuals dialog box will open.

OR

9b. **Click** on **No**. The two individuals will not be merged.

NOTE

You will have another opportunity to verify that the two individuals are the same. If they are, click on the Merge button. If they are not, click on the Cancel button.

Using Global Find and Replace

There will be times when you will discover that you have consistently misspelled a word or phrase. The Find and Replace feature allows you to have Family Tree Maker search for the wrong word or phrase and replace it with the correct one.

1. Click on the **Family Page button**. The Family Page will appear.

2. Click on **Edit**. The Edit menu will appear.

3. Click on **Find and Replace**. The Find and Replace dialog box will open.

4. In the Find field, **enter** the **word or phrase** you want to find.

5. In the Replace with field, **type** the **word or phrase** with which you want to replace it.

6. Click on **Find**. The Find and Replace dialog box will show the first match.

7a. Click on **Find Next**. Family Tree Maker will ignore the current occurrence and look for the next match.

OR

7b. Click on **Replace All**. Family Tree Maker will replace all occurrences of the Find word with the Replace with word.

OR

7c. Click on **Replace**. Family Tree Maker will replace just that particular occurrence of the Find word with the Replace with word.

8. Click on **Close**. Family Tree Maker will close the Find and Replace dialog box.

Part III Review Questions

1. How can you access the Index of Individuals? *See "Using Quick Search by Name" in Chapter 10*

2. What are the ways you can arrange the Index of Individuals? *See "Rearranging the Index" in Chapter 10*

3. What are the other ways you can search for an individual in your Family File? *See "Using the Find Individual Feature" in Chapter 10*

4. How can you do online research using Family Tree Maker? *See "Working with the FamilyFinder Center" in Chapter 10*

5. What are the two ways you can run the spell checker in Family Tree Maker? *See "Working with the Family Tree Maker Spelling Checker" in Chapter 11*

6. How can you delete an individual from your Family File? *See "Deleting One Person" in Chapter 11*

7. What are the three ways you can check your Family File for errors? *See "Checking the Family File for Errors" in Chapter 11*

8. How can you link a previously entered child to previously entered parents? *See "Linking Children to Their Parents" in Chapter 12*

9. What are two ways you can merge duplicate individuals in your Family File? *See "Fixing Duplicates" in Chapter 12*

10. How can you do a global find and replace of a word or phrase? *See "Using Global Find and Replace" in Chapter 12*

PART IV

Visualizing Your Family in Family Tree Maker

13

Understanding Tree Reports in Family Tree Maker

After you have entered information about your family into Family Tree Maker, it is natural for you to want to display that information in different formats. Family Tree Maker offers a number of different trees that will show you ancestors, descendants, or both for a selected individual. In this chapter, you'll learn how to:

- Display Ancestor Trees
- Display Hourglass Trees
- Display Descendant Trees
- Display All-in-One Trees
- Enhance the tree views

Displaying Ancestor Trees

The Ancestor Trees allow you to see how many direct line generations you have been able to carry your research back from a selected individual. Family Tree Maker offers three different versions of the Ancestor Tree.

Creating Fan Charts

The Fan Chart of an Ancestor Tree begins with the selected individual. It then displays all the ancestors: parents, grandparents, great-grandparents, and so on. You can control how the chart looks and how many generations to include.

1. Click on the **Ancestor Tree button**. The Ancestor Tree menu will appear.

2. Click on **Fan**. The Fan Chart will appear.

TIP

Family Tree Maker allows you to change the format of the chart using the toolbar along the right side of the tree.

3. Click on the **Format button**. The Format for Ancestor Tree dialog box will open.

4. Select the **Custom radio button**. All the options will be enabled.

5. Select the **shape** of the Fan Chart.

6. Select the **density** of the Fan Chart.

7. Click on **OK**. The Format for Ancestor Tree dialog box will close and your changes will be saved.

NOTE

Throughout this chapter, you will examine all the different toolbar buttons as you learn about each tree.

Creating a Pedigree Chart

The pedigree chart is the standard chart used by genealogists. This chart is a road map of your direct lineage and usually displays from four to six generations per page.

1. Click on the **Ancestor Tree button**. The Ancestor Tree menu will appear.

2. Click on **Standard**. The Standard Pedigree Chart will appear.

3. Click on the **Format button**. The Tree Format for Ancestor Tree dialog box will open.

4. Select the **type of Ancestor Tree** you want to display.

5. Select the **type of connections** you want to use in the chart. The chart's boxes will be moved closer together or further apart, depending on the type of connections you select.

NOTE

The Layout options are only active when you select the Custom type.

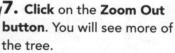

TIP

When you select the Book layout type, you can elect to have each tree centered on the page.

6. Click on **OK**. The Tree Format for Ancestor Tree dialog box will close and your changes will be saved.

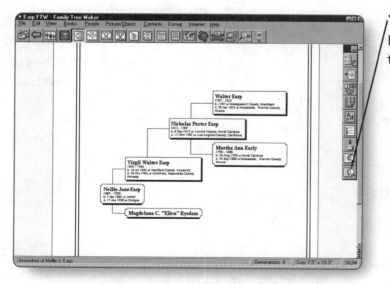

7. Click on the **Zoom Out button**. You will see more of the tree.

Rearranging the Standard Ancestor Chart

While the Ancestor Tree is a standard form, better known as a pedigree chart, many researchers find that they like to customize the chart. In addition to the methods mentioned above, you can also move individual boxes or a complete lineage using your mouse and the keyboard.

TIP

You must be in the Custom format to rearrange the tree.

1a. **Click** on the **individual** whose lineage you want to move. The individual and his or her lineage will be selected.

OR

1b. **Hold** down the **CTRL key** while you **click** on the **individual** you want to move. The individual will be selected.

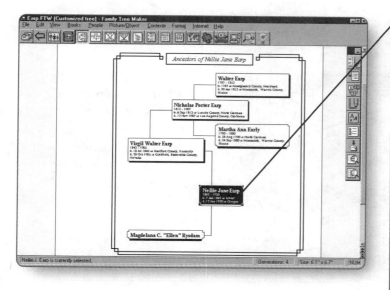

2. Drag the **mouse** to the new location. The individual or the selected lineage will be moved to the selected location.

NOTE

Remember that when you are dragging the mouse, it is necessary to hold down the left mouse button or the left mouse button and the CTRL key to achieve the desired effect.

Creating a Vertical Ancestor Tree

The Vertical Ancestor Tree is a box-style chart. It starts at the bottom of a page or set of pages and goes up, showing the ancestors of the selected individual.

1. Click on the **Ancestor Tree button**. The Ancestor Tree menu will appear.

2. Click on **Vertical**. The Vertical Ancestor Tree will appear.

3. Click on the **Items to**

TIP

You can change what information is included in the boxes for each of the individuals.

Include button. The Items to Include in Ancestor Tree dialog box will open.

4. Click on an **item** in the Available items list.

5. Click on the **inclusion button.** The Options dialog box will open.

6. Click on the **options** for the selected item. A check mark will appear next to the options selected.

7. Click on **OK.** The Options dialog box will close and the item will appear in the The boxes in your tree contain these items list.

NOTE

The choices in the Options dialog box will vary depending on the item you selected from the Available items list.

8. Click on an **item** in the The boxes in your tree contain these items list. The item will be selected.

9. Click on the **Move up or Move down button**. The item will be moved to a new position.

10. Click on **OK**. The changes will be applied to the Vertical Ancestor Tree.

NOTE

The order in which the items appear in the The boxes in your tree contain these items list is the order in which they will appear in the boxes of the tree.

Displaying Hourglass Trees

The Hourglass Tree allows you to view not only the ancestors but also the descendants of the selected individual. The individual is in the center with the ancestors opening above and the descendants opening below, looking much like an hourglass.

Working with the Fan Format

Like other fan-styled trees, the Hourglass Tree in fan format takes advantage of the fan shape. Keep in mind that with a large lineage, the fan style will use up a lot of paper when you print it.

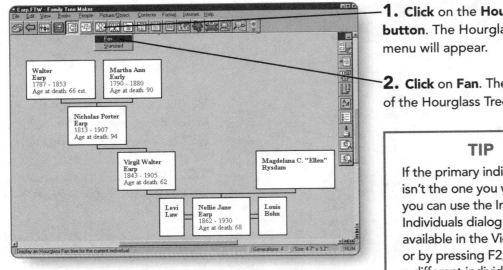

1. **Click** on the **Hourglass Tree button**. The Hourglass Tree menu will appear.

2. **Click** on **Fan**. The fan format of the Hourglass Tree will appear.

> ### TIP
>
> If the primary individual isn't the one you want, you can use the Index of Individuals dialog box, available in the View menu or by pressing F2, to select a different individual. See Chapter 10, "Searching Your Family Tree File," to review how to do this.

3. **Click** on the **Number of Generations button**. The # of Generations to Show dialog box will open.

4. **Use** the **arrows** to select the number of ancestors and descendants desired.

5. **Click** on **OK**. The # of Generations to Show dialog box will close.

Working with Standard Format

The standard format of the Hourglass Tree uses a box chart. The boxes can be as large or as small as you want, depending on the information you include.

1. Click on the **Hourglass Tree button**. The Hourglass Tree menu will appear.

2. Click on **Standard**. The standard format of the Hourglass Tree will appear.

TIP

You can determine the events and comments included in each box; simply click on the Items to Include button.

3. Click on the **Box, Line, & Border Styles button**. The Styles for Hourglass Tree dialog box will open.

4a. **Click** on the **Boxes tab** to access style and color options for the boxes.

OR

4b. **Click** on the **Borders tab** to access style and color options for the border of the tree.

OR

4c. **Click** on the **Lines tab** to access style and color options for the lines connecting the boxes.

NOTE

Each of these sections uses buttons and drop-down menus to make the options available.

Including Siblings on Trees

Once in a while you might want to get a good overall view of your data with more than just the direct ancestral lineage. Taking advantage of the option to include siblings is one way to do that. Before beginning these steps, make sure you have the Vertical Ancestor Tree open.

NOTE

While this example concentrates on the Vertical Ancestor Tree, this option is available for all of the Ancestor Tree formats, as well as for the Standard Hourglass Tree.

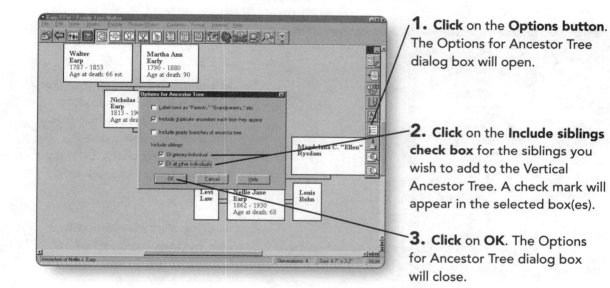

1. Click on the **Options button**. The Options for Ancestor Tree dialog box will open.

2. Click on the **Include siblings check box** for the siblings you wish to add to the Vertical Ancestor Tree. A check mark will appear in the selected box(es).

3. Click on **OK**. The Options for Ancestor Tree dialog box will close.

Notice how the changes affect the overall look of the Vertical Ancestor Tree, especially if you have elected to include the siblings for everyone on the tree.

Displaying Descendant Trees

There will be times when you want to view the descendants of a given ancestor. Some research projects will require tracing the children and grandchildren. Descendant Trees allow you to see these in an easy-to-read format.

Creating a Standard Tree

As with the other trees you have looked at, there is a standard format of the Descendant Tree. This standard tree is often known as a box chart. It details the descendants of a selected individual.

1. Click on the **Descendant Tree button**. The Descendant Tree menu will appear.

2. Click on **Standard**. The standard format of the Descendant Tree will appear.

TIP

You can rearrange the shape of the Standard Descendant Tree by clicking and dragging, as you did with the Standard Ancestor Tree earlier in this chapter.

Creating an Outline Tree

When you're working with the descendants of a given individual, Family Tree Maker offers an outline, or indented, tree. Each generation is indented, making it easy to distinguish each generation from the others.

1. Click on the **Outline Descendant Tree button.** The Outline Report will appear.

2. Click on the **Format button.** The Tree Format for Outline Descendant Tree dialog box will open.

NOTE

This dialog box allows you to change the indent character as well as the size and spacing.

3. Click on **OK**. The Tree Format for Outline Descendant Tree dialog box will close.

Displaying All-in-One Trees

There will be times when you will want to view all the individuals in your database. Family Tree Maker makes this possible with the All-in-One Tree.

Creating an All-in-One Tree

An All-in-One Tree is easily created because Family Tree Maker does all the hard work.

1. Click on the **All-in-One Tree button**. The All-in-One Tree will appear.

2. Click on the **Options button**. The Options for All-in-One Tree dialog box will open.

NOTE

The dotted lines you see on the All-in-One Tree display the page margins. The All-in-One Tree will require multiple pages when printed, and those pages will then need to be taped together.

TIP

The Unconnected Branches check boxes allow you to include or exclude unconnected lines that have been entered in your database.

3. Choose your desired **settings** and **click** on **OK**. The Options for All-in-One Tree dialog box will close.

Setting Display Size

Because the All-in-One Tree displays all the individuals in your database, its size can be cumbersome. Customizing the display size can make it easier to understand the true scope of this view.

1. Click on the **Zoom In button**. The All-in-One view will zoom in.

2. Use the **scroll bar** to move the All-in-One Tree to see the boxes not currently on the screen.

TIP

You can also use the View menu to select the Zoom options. To see the entire All-in-One Tree, choose Size to Window.

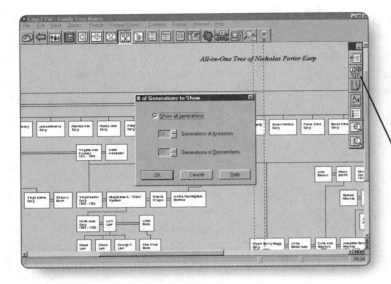

Pruning the Display

In addition to excluding the unrelated trees, you can control the number of generations included in your tree.

1. Click on the **Number of Generations button**. The # of Generations to Show dialog box will open.

2. Click on the **Show all generations check box** to clear it.

3. Use the **arrows** in the Generations of Ancestors field to select the number of generations of ancestors you want to show.

4. Use the **arrows** in the Generations of Descendants field to select the number of generations of descendants you want to show.

5. Click on **OK**. The # of Generations to Show dialog box will close and the changes will appear on the tree.

Enhancing the Tree Views

There are different ways to enhance the appearance of the different trees. With colors and different box styles, you can make different lineages or genders stand out.

Emphasizing Relationships

With line styles and colors, you can make a particular relationship clearer on your tree.

1. **Click** on the **Box, Line, & Border Styles button**. The Styles dialog box will open.

> **NOTE**
>
> The exact name of the Styles dialog box will vary, depending on what type of tree you are creating.

2. **Click** on the **Lines tab**. The Lines tab will move to the front.

3. **Click** on the **Highlight the relationship between check box** to select or deselect it. A check mark will appear when you select this option and will disappear when you deselect it.

4. **Click** on the **Change button** to change one of the individuals currently selected. The Index of Individuals dialog box will open and will include a list of only those individuals already included in the tree.

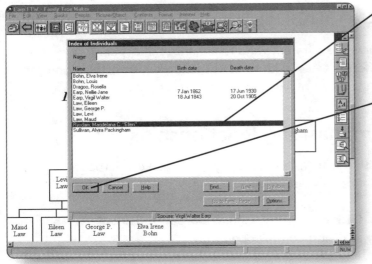

5. Click on the desired **individual** in the list. The selected individual will be highlighted.

6. Click on **OK**. The Index of Individuals dialog box will close.

7. Click on the **Line color down arrow**. The Line color drop-down menu will appear.

8. Click on a **color**. The color will be selected.

9. Click on **OK**. The Styles dialog box will close and your changes will be saved.

Adding a Background Image

There is nothing more interesting than enhancing the overall appearance of your tree. This can be done effectively by placing a picture in the background.

1. Click on **Picture/Object**. The Picture/Object menu will appear.

2. Click on **Tree Background Picture**. The Background Picture dialog box will open.

3. Click on the **Display picture in background check box**. The option will be selected.

4. Click on the **Choose button**. The Insert Picture window will open so you can select a picture.

TIP

After selecting a digitized picture, you might want to fade the picture so that it does not make reading the tree difficult. The smaller the number in the Fade Picture field, the more faint the picture will appear behind the chart, making the chart easier to read.

5. Click on **OK**. The Background Picture dialog box will close and the picture will appear in the background of the tree.

14

Working with Reports

In addition to its many trees, Family Tree Maker also includes a number of other reports that allow you to understand what you have in your database and how the individuals might be related. In this chapter, you'll learn how to:

- Create a Custom Report
- Create a Kinship Report
- Create an Address Report
- Create a Birthday Report
- Use the Research Journal

Creating a Custom Report

Just as the name implies, Custom Reports allow you to control the individuals and information included in the reports.

1. Click on the **Report button**. The Report window will appear.

2. Click on the **Report Format button**. The Report Format dialog box will open.

3. Click on **Custom Report** in the Select a format for your report list.

4. Click on **OK**. The Report Format dialog box will close.

Adding Items to Include in Your Report

The Custom Report might not have in it the information you want to include. However, this report is easy to adjust.

1. Click on the **Items to Include button**. The Items to Include in Report dialog box will open.

2. In the Available items list, **click** on an **item** that you want to include.

3. Click on the **inclusion button**. The Options dialog box might open, depending on the item you've chosen to include.

NOTE

Not all of the Items to Include options will have detailed options. When there are no available options, the Options dialog box will not open.

4. Select the desired **options**. A check mark will appear next to the options you have selected.

5. Click on **OK**. The Options dialog box will close and the items you selected will be included in the Each row of your report will contain list.

Choosing Individuals to Include in Your Report

You might want to limit the individuals appearing in the report if you do not want to show your entire database. You can do this individually or by relationship.

1. **Click** on the **Individuals to Include button**. The Include dialog box will open.

2. **Click** on the **Selected individuals** radio button. The option will be selected.

3. **Click** on the **Individuals to Include button**. The Individuals to Include dialog box will open.

4. In the Available individuals list, **select** the **individual** you want to include.

5. Click on the appropriate **inclusion button**. The individual you selected (and his or her ancestors or descendants, if applicable) will be moved to the You have included these individuals list.

NOTE

There are four major inclusion buttons. The [>] button tells Family Tree Maker to include the single highlighted individual. The [>>] button will include all the individuals. The Ancestors button will include the ancestors of the highlighted individual. The Descendants button will include the descendants of the highlighted individual.

TIP

To learn how to use the Find button to determine the individuals you want to include in the list, see Chapter 22, "Working with Custom Reports and Research Journal Features."

6. Click on **OK**. The Individuals to Include dialog box will close and your changes will be saved.

Creating a Title and Footnote

If you will be supplying this report to others, you might want to give it a title and include a footnote that will appear on each page.

1. Click on **Contents**. The Contents menu will appear.

2. Click on **Title & Footnote**. The Title & Footnote for Report dialog box will open.

3. Click on a **radio button** to select the appropriate title option.

4. Select the desired **page number, date, and time options**.

5. Type a **footnote** in the Footnote field.

6. Click on **OK**. The Title & Footnote for Report dialog box will close.

Adjusting Column Widths

Sometimes, in an effort to fit as much information in a report as possible, it is necessary to adjust the column widths.

1. Click on **Format**. The Format menu will appear.

2. Click on **Maximum Width for each Column**. The Maximum Width for Each Column dialog box will open.

3a. Click on the **Set widths automatically radio button**. The option will be selected.

OR

3b. Click on the **Choose widths manually radio button**. The option will be selected.

4. If you chose to adjust the widths manually, **adjust** the **width and spacing** for each column.

TIP

Pay close attention to the total report width. This lets you know how much space your columns will take up on the page.

---

5. Click on **OK**. The Maximum Width for Each Column dialog box will close.

Sorting Reports

One benefit of putting this information into a database is that it gives you the ability to manipulate the data after it has been entered. You can sort the report based on the columns included.

1. Click on **Format**. The Format menu will appear.

2. Click on **Sort Report**. The Sort Report dialog box will open.

3. From the Sort by drop-down menu, **select** the **first column** by which you want to sort.

4a. Click on the **Ascending radio button** to sort in ascending order.

OR

4b. Click on the **Descending radio button** to sort in descending order.

5. From the Then by drop-down menu, **select** the **second column** by which you want to sort, if desired.

6. Click on **OK**. The Sort Report dialog box will close.

Creating a Kinship Report

Kinship Reports help you determine just how individuals in your database are related. The people making up several generations might be related in more than one way.

1. Click on **Format**. The Format menu will appear.

2. Click on **Report Format**. The Report Format dialog box will open.

3. Click on **Kinship - Relationship Only** in the Select a format for your report list. The Kinship - Relationship Only report will be selected.

4. Click on **OK**. The Report Format dialog box will close.

TIP

Remember that you can change the primary individual. Press F2 or click on the Index of Individuals button to open the Index of Individuals and select the person you want as the primary individual.

Working with Address and Birthday Reports

Whether you find yourself the keeper of addresses for the family association or you just want to print out a report of birthdays so you will be sure to send cards, Family Tree Maker kept you in mind.

Creating an Address Report

If you have taken advantage of the More About Address option for living individuals, you can print out a report with those addresses.

1. Open the **Report Format dialog box**, as you did in the previous section, "Creating a Kinship Report."

2. Click on **Address** in the Select a format for your report list. The Address Report will be selected.

3. Click on **OK**. The Report Format dialog box will close.

TIP
You can determine which individuals are included in the Address Report. Simply click on the Individuals to Include button.

NOTE
You might have some unexpected individuals in your report. Individuals can "inherit" an address if one has been entered for a parent or spouse.

Creating the Birthday Report

Thanks to the Birthday Report, you no longer need to look through all the pages of your living family members to find birthdays. The Birthday Report can display the birthdays of all the living individuals in your database, or it can show just those you want to select.

1. Click on the **Report Format button**. The Report Format dialog box will open.

2. Select the **Birthdays of Living Individuals** report from the Select a format for your report list.

3. Click on **OK**.

The Report Format dialog box will close and the Birthday Report will be displayed.

NOTE
Family Tree Maker omits anyone with a death date and anyone who is over 120 years old.

Using the Research Journal

The Research Journal offers a means for tracking your past research and for making notes on future research.

1. Click on the **FamilyFinder Center button**. The FamilyFinder Center will appear.

2. Click on **My Research Journal/To-Do List**. The Research Journal screen will appear.

3. Click on the **Click here to create a new to-do item link** to add a To-Do item. The New To-Do Item dialog box will open.

> ### NOTE
> For more information on working with the Research Journal, see Chapter 22, "Working with Custom Reports and Research Journal Features."

4. Enter a **description** of what you want to accomplish in the To-Do field.

5. Click on the **arrows** in the Priority field to select a priority.

> ### TIP
> You can use the Category field to organize your To-Do items under categories such as Census or Church Records.

6. Click on **OK**. The New To-Do Item dialog box will close.

Working with the Genealogy How-To Guide

Whether you are just beginning or you have been involved for a while in researching your family history, there will be times when you will have questions about where to go with your research.

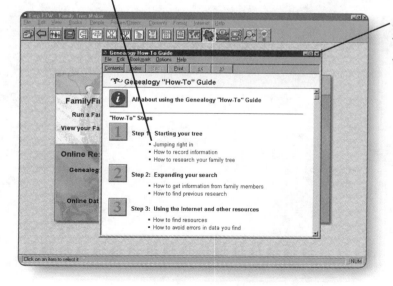

1. Click on the **FamilyFinder Center button**. The FamilyFinder Center will appear.

2. Click on **How to Get Started**. The Genealogy "How-To" Guide window will appear.

3. Click on an **item of interest**. Further instructions will appear.

4. Click on the **Close button**. The Genealogy "How-To" Guide window will close.

15

Viewing and Printing Reports and Trees

Now that you have learned how to enter information and view some of the reports and trees, you're probably very interested in learning how to format them and print them out. In this chapter, you'll learn how to:

- View the tree you want to print
- Customize the view of the tree
- Change the print setup
- Print the tree

Viewing the Tree You Want to Print

Family Tree Maker assumes that the tree or report you are interested in is the one on the screen, so you need to display the tree to print it.

1. Click on the **tree view** you want to print. A menu might appear, depending on which tree view you select.

2. If a menu does appear, **click** on the **tree type** you want to print. The tree will appear.

Customizing the View

After you have displayed the tree you want to print, you can fine-tune the text style, font, and size. These features will only appear when the tree is printed.

1. Click on the **Text Font, Style, & Size button**. The Text Font, Style, & Size dialog box will open.

NOTE

The complete name of the dialog box will depend on the tree or report that you have selected.

Changing the Text Font

One wonderful aspect of computers and modern printers is that you can be creative with the fonts you use. You can go from formal to fun.

1. **Click** on an **item** in the Items to format list.

2. **Click** on the **Font down arrow**. The Font drop-down menu will appear.

3. **Click** on the **font** you want to use. The font will be selected.

NOTE

Use the scroll bar to view the list of fonts.

TIP

If you use the keyboard arrow keys to move through the list of fonts, you will see a sample of each font in the Sample box.

Working with Text Style

In order to make things stand out, you might want to change the style of the text. For instance, you might decide that you want to italicize the dates to call attention to them.

1. Select an **item** to format from the Items to format list.

2. Click on the **Style down arrow.** The Style drop-down menu will appear.

3. Click on the desired **style.** The style will be selected and the drop-down menu will close.

NOTE

If you want more than one item to have this style, press the Ctrl key and click on the additional items in the Items to format list. Then select the style from the Style drop-down menu.

Working with Text Size

Family Tree Maker has developed a number of default sizes for the fonts used in reports. You can change these if you want to, but in some cases it might make your report much larger.

1. Select an **item** to format from the Items to format list.

2. Click on the **Size down arrow**. The Size drop-down menu will appear.

3. Click on the desired **size**. The size will be selected.

TIP

You can change the font, size, and style of an item all at once. Just select the item from the Items to format list and make your desired changes.

Working with Text Color

If you are going to a family reunion or some other gathering where you want your chart to look extra-special, you will want to take advantage of the color options Family Tree Maker offers.

1. Select an **item** to format from the Items to format list.

2. Click on the **Color down arrow**. The Color drop-down menu will appear.

3. Click on the desired **color**. The color will be selected.

Changing the Print Setup

Family Tree Maker uses your Windows printer settings, but you might want to change those settings if you are not happy with the way a particular report is printing.

Changing the Paper Orientation

There are two ways to print on a piece of paper. Portrait uses paper in the standard 8.5-by-11-inch mode; Landscape uses paper in 11-by-8.5-inch mode.

1. Click on **File**. The File menu will appear.

2. Click on **Print Setup**. The Print Setup dialog box will open.

NOTE

The full name of this dialog box will differ depending on the report or tree you have selected.

3. Click on the **Portrait radio button**, if it is not already selected. The option will be selected.

4. Click on the **Landscape radio button**. The option will be selected and the sample paper icon will change to reflect the Landscape orientation.

Adjusting Margins

Usually the margins that have been set are at the optimum range for the reports and the printer used. However, you can change them.

1. In the Print Setup dialog box, **click** on the **up and down arrows** to adjust the Top, Bottom, Left, and Right margins.

TIP

If you're printing one of the Box Charts or Fan Charts that will use more than one piece of paper, you will want to turn on the Overlap pages option. This makes it easier to line up the pages when you are putting the printed chart together.

Changing Other Settings

There might be a time when you will want to adjust the features of your printer. This is especially useful when you're printing reports that have scanned images, because you can tell the printer to print at its peak quality for that report.

1. In the Print Setup dialog box, **click** on the **Options button**. The printer Properties dialog box will open.

2. Make the desired **changes** to the printing quality and other printing options.

3. Click on **OK**. The Properties dialog box will close.

4. Click on **OK**. The Print Setup dialog box will close.

Printing the Tree

After you have made the necessary changes to the printer setup and you have formatted your tree the way you want, it is time to print it.

1. Click on **File**. The File menu will appear.

2. Click on **Print Tree**. The Print Tree dialog box will open.

NOTE

The actual name of the Print Tree dialog box will vary depending on the report selected.

3. In the Copies field, **enter** the **number of copies** you want to print.

4. Select the **Print empty check box** to print an empty report.

5. Select the **Print color check box** to print the report in color, if you have a color printer.

NOTE

Printing an empty report is an excellent way to have needed forms when you are on a research trip.

6a. **Click** on **OK**. The report will be sent to the printer.

OR

6b. **Click** on **Cancel**. The report will not be printed.

16

Creating Genealogy Style and Genealogical Source Reports

After you have entered all your information, you will want to share it with family members and other researchers. The Genealogy Style Reports are one of the best ways to do this. In this chapter, you'll learn how to:

- Select a genealogy style
- Include sources as endnotes in reports
- Format the report
- Locate conflicting data
- Create a Bibliography Report
- Create a Documented Events Report

Using Genealogy Style Reports

Genealogy Reports in Family Tree Maker are narrative reports containing genealogical information, basic facts, and biographical details. These are the most common formats you see in published family histories.

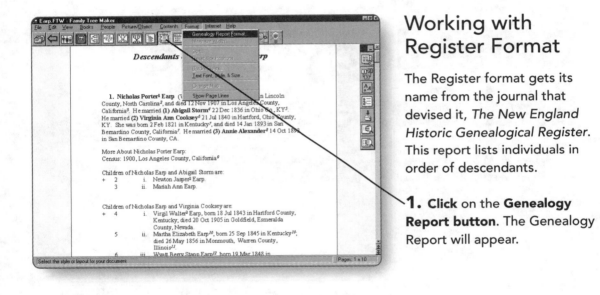

Working with Register Format

The Register format gets its name from the journal that devised it, *The New England Historic Genealogical Register*. This report lists individuals in order of descendants.

1. Click on the **Genealogy Report button**. The Genealogy Report will appear.

2. Click on **Format**. The Format menu will appear.

3. Click on **Genealogy Report Format**. The Genealogy Report Format dialog box will open.

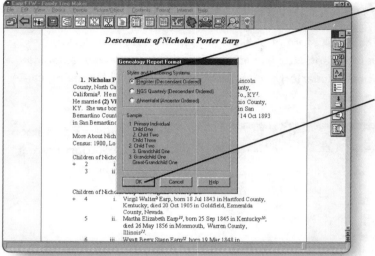

4. Click on the **Register (Descendant Ordered) radio button**. The option will be selected.

5. Click on **OK**. The Genealogy Report Format dialog box will close.

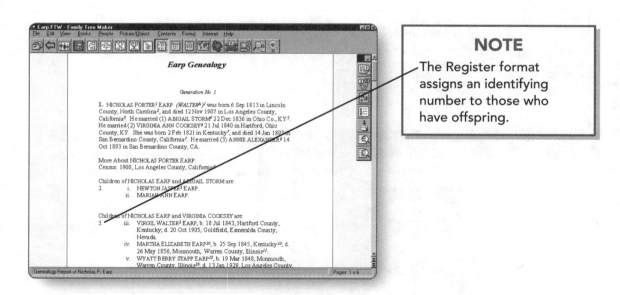

NOTE

The Register format assigns an identifying number to those who have offspring.

Working with NGSQ Format

The NGSQ format also displays individuals in order of descendants. It was named after the *National Genealogical Society Quarterly,* the journal of the National Genealogical Society.

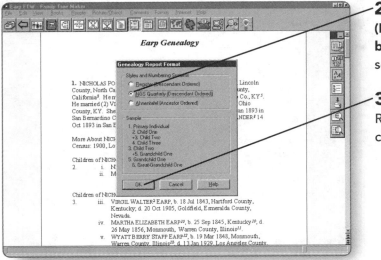

1. Click on the **Format button**. The Genealogy Report Format dialog box will open.

2. Click on the **NGS Quarterly (Descendant Ordered) radio button**. The option will be selected.

3. Click on **OK**. The Genealogy Report Format dialog box will close.

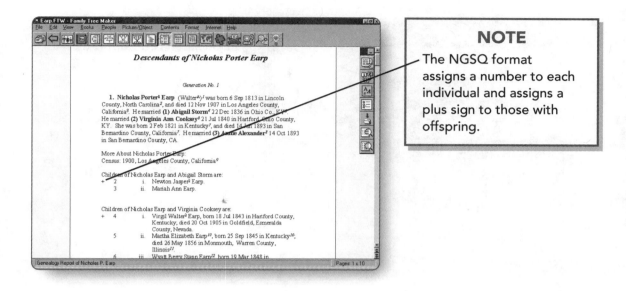

NOTE

The NGSQ format assigns a number to each individual and assigns a plus sign to those with offspring.

Using the Ahnentafel Report

Ahnentafel is a German word that means "ancestor table" or "family table." This report lists individuals in an ancestral order. This is the opposite of the other two reports.

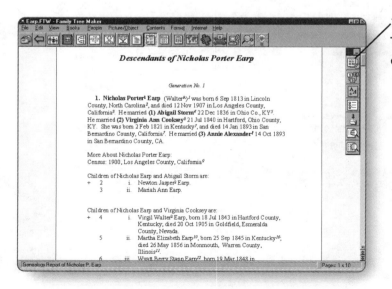

1. Click on the **Format button**. The Genealogy Report Format dialog box will open.

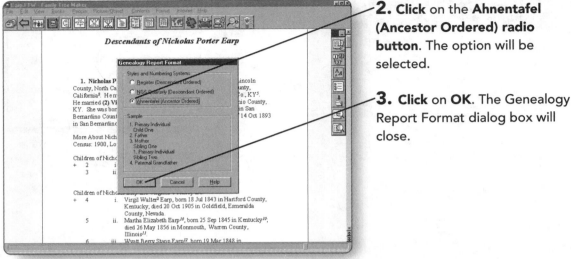

2. Click on the **Ahnentafel (Ancestor Ordered) radio button**. The option will be selected.

3. Click on **OK**. The Genealogy Report Format dialog box will close.

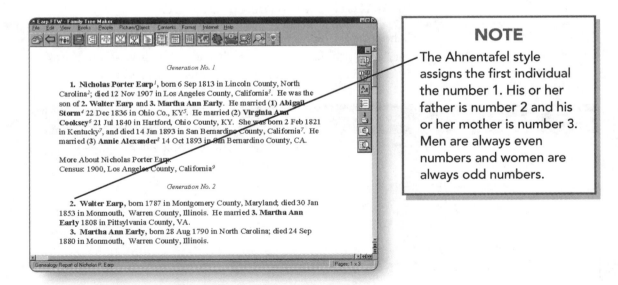

NOTE

The Ahnentafel style assigns the first individual the number 1. His or her father is number 2 and his or her mother is number 3. Men are always even numbers and women are always odd numbers.

Using Endnotes

Genealogy Style Reports include source citations. These can be included in the body of the report or they can be printed as endnotes.

1. Click on the **Options button**. The Options for Genealogy Report dialog box will open.

2. Click on the **Include source information as endnotes radio button**. The option will be selected.

3. Click on **OK**. The Options for Genealogy Report dialog box will close.

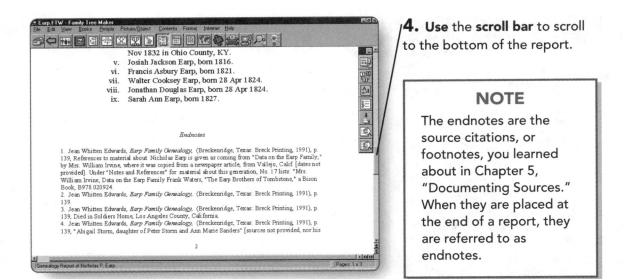

4. Use the **scroll bar** to scroll to the bottom of the report.

NOTE

The endnotes are the source citations, or footnotes, you learned about in Chapter 5, "Documenting Sources." When they are placed at the end of a report, they are referred to as endnotes.

Formatting the Report

In addition to the different styles of reports, there are other items that need to be considered, such as page numbering and the type of notes to include.

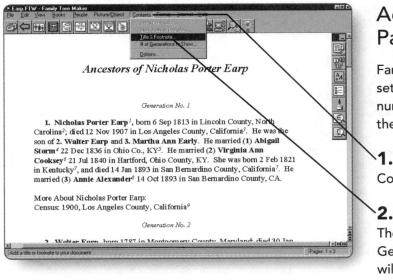

Adjusting Title and Page Numbering

Family Tree Maker has default settings for the title and page number, but you can change these settings.

1. Click on **Contents**. The Contents menu will appear.

2. Click on **Title & Footnote**. The Title & Footnote for Genealogy Report dialog box will open.

NOTE

All of the reports allow for title and footnote options. The title of this dialog box will vary depending on which type of report or tree you are using.

3a. **Click** on the **Automatic title radio button**. The option will be selected.

OR

3b. **Click** on the **Custom title radio button**. The cursor will move to the empty field, where you can type the title as you want it to display in the report.

4. In the Page Number and Date section, **click** on the **page number and date options** you want to set.

5. **Use** the **up and down arrows** in the Starting number field to change the starting page number.

6. **Click** on **OK**. The Title & Footnote for Genealogy Report dialog box will close.

Changing the Number of Generations

As you can with the trees, you can control the number of generations that are included in the Genealogy Report.

1. **Click** on the **Number of Generations button**. The # of Generations to Show for Genealogy Report dialog box will open.

2. **Use** the **up and down arrows** in the Select number of generations to show field to adjust the number.

TIP

The number in the Select number of generations to show field is highlighted when the dialog box is opened, so you can just type the number of generations to include in the report if you prefer not to use the up and down arrows.

---

3. **Click** on **OK**. The # of Generations to Show for Genealogy Report dialog box will close.

Including Notes and Other Options

In Chapter 7, "Understanding More About Notes," you learned to include family stories. These stories can be included in printed reports.

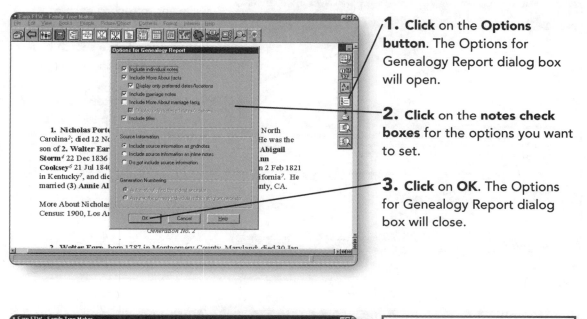

1. Click on the **Options button**. The Options for Genealogy Report dialog box will open.

2. Click on the **notes check boxes** for the options you want to set.

3. Click on **OK**. The Options for Genealogy Report dialog box will close.

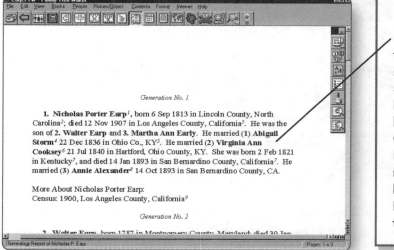

TIP

It is a good idea to read through the report to see if the notes are appropriate and should be included. Even if you have not opened the Options for Genealogy Report dialog box, some notes will be included because Family Tree Maker has note options turned on by default.

Locating Conflicting Facts

Family Tree Maker allows you to enter duplicate facts. This is by design, because you will find dates in your research that conflict with each other and you will want to record each of them. Family Tree Maker also lets you conduct a search based on these conflicting facts.

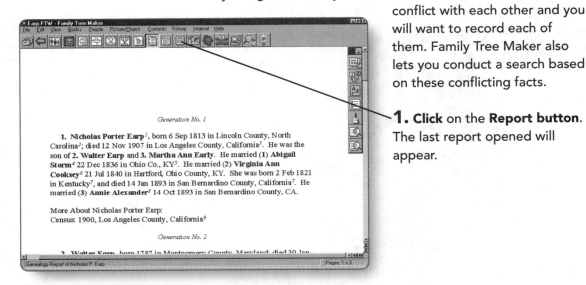

1. Click on the **Report button**. The last report opened will appear.

2. Click on the **Format button**. The Report Format dialog box will open.

3. Scroll down until you reach the bottom of the Select a format for your report list.

4. Click on **Alternate Facts**. The option will be selected.

5. Click on **OK**. The Report Format dialog box will close.

6. Click on an **individual** in the report. The individual will be selected.

7. Click on **View**. The View menu will appear.

8. Move the **mouse pointer** to More About. The More About menu will appear.

9. Click on **Facts**. The More About Facts window will appear, so you can view the facts for the individual.

Creating a Bibliography Report

A bibliography is a list of books and sources. These are the sources you have used to compile your Family File. A Bibliography Report is a useful reference tool.

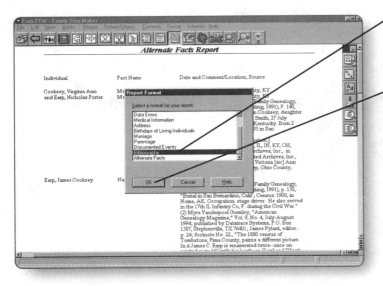

1. Click on the **Report button**. The Report will appear.

2. Click on the **Format button**. The Report Format dialog box will open.

3. Click on **Bibliography** in the Select a format for your report list. The option will be selected.

4. Click on **OK**. The Report Format dialog box will close.

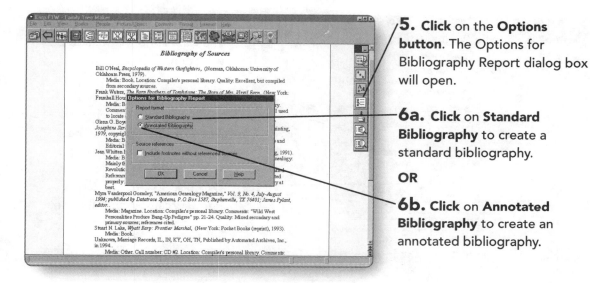

5. **Click** on the **Options button**. The Options for Bibliography Report dialog box will open.

6a. **Click** on **Standard Bibliography** to create a standard bibliography.

OR

6b. **Click** on **Annotated Bibliography** to create an annotated bibliography.

NOTE

An annotated bibliography includes the full source citation and comments by the researcher about the source.

Creating a Documented Events Report

Understanding how you came to the conclusions you did in your Family File is usually directly related to the sources used. The Documented Events Report is a clear list of the individuals and events you have documented.

1. Click on the **Format button**. The Report Format dialog box will open.

2. In the Select a format for your report list, **click** on **Documented Events**. The option will be selected.

3. Click on **OK**. The Report Format dialog box will close.

4. Click on the **Options button**. The Options for Documented Events Report dialog box will open.

5. Click on the desired **Whom to report radio button**. The option will be selected.

6. Click on the desired **What to report radio button**. The option will be selected.

7. Click on **OK**. The Options for Documented Events Report dialog box will close.

Part IV Review Questions

1. What three types of Ancestor Trees can you display?
   See "Displaying Ancestor Trees" in Chapter 13

2. Which Descendant Tree indents the individuals?
   See "Creating an Outline Tree" in Chapter 13

3. How do you view a complete All-in-One Tree?
   See "Setting Display Size" in Chapter 13

4. How do you select the items to include in a Custom Report?
   See "Adding Items to Include in Your Report" in Chapter 14

5. How can you record plans for future research?
   See "Using the Research Journal" in Chapter 14

6. Where can you turn for guidance in your research?
   See "Working with the Genealogy How-To Guide" in Chapter 14

7. How do you alter the overall feel of the trees in Family Tree Maker?
   See "Customizing the View" in Chapter 15

8. Can you print in both Landscape and Portrait modes?
   See "Changing the Paper Orientation" in Chapter 15

9. What three types of Genealogy Reports are available?
   See "Using Genealogy Style Reports" in Chapter 16

10. Can you create a bibliography of the sources used in your research?
    See "Creating a Bibliography Report" in Chapter 16

PART V

Publishing Your Family History

17

Creating a Scrapbook

Using present technology, it is possible to create beautiful reports and enhance them by adding scanned and digitized photographs. Family Tree Maker calls these reports *scrapbooks*. In this chapter, you'll learn how to:

- Use a scrapbook
- Insert images into a scrapbook
- Enter information about scrapbook items
- Rearrange scrapbook objects
- Edit pictures or objects
- Search for objects
- Share your scrapbook

Using the Scrapbook

The scrapbook is where you can work with digitized files such as scanned photographs. There are scrapbooks for individuals and for marriages.

1. Click on the **Family Page button**. The Family Page will appear.

2. Click on the **Scrapbk button**.

The Individual Scrapbook window will appear. Each frame can hold a digitized image, sound clip, or other object.

Inserting Scrapbook Objects

While most of the items you will work with will be scanned photographs, Family Tree Maker does support sound clips and OLE (*Object Linking and Embedding*) objects.

Using Graphics Images

Scanning photographs helps to preserve them, and they can then be included in the reports you print from Family Tree Maker. But first you need to import the image files.

1. Click on **Picture/Object**. The Picture/Object menu will appear.

2. Click on **Insert Picture from File**. The Insert Picture dialog box will open.

TIP

It is also possible to scan the picture directly into the scrapbook. Click on Insert Picture from Scanner/Camera. Remember, though, that images can take up a great deal of space on your hard drive. For scanned images, it is recommended that you set the resolution to a maximum of 200 DPI (*Dots Per Inch*). This will produce a good picture and keep the file size down at the same time.

3. Use the **Look in drop-down menu** to locate the folder that holds the images.

4. Click on the desired **image**. The image will be selected.

5. Click on **Open**. The Insert Picture dialog box will close and the picture will appear in the Edit Picture dialog box.

6. Click on **OK**. The Edit Picture dialog box will close.

Using Sound Clips

There is something fascinating about hearing the voice of a relative. Family Tree Maker offers a way of including sound clips in the scrapbook.

1. Click on **Picture/Object**. The Picture/Object menu will appear.

2. Click on **Insert Object**. The Insert Object dialog box will open.

3. Click on the **Create from File radio button**. The option will be selected.

4. Click on the **Browse button**. The Browse dialog box will open.

5. Use the **Look in drop-down menu** to locate the proper folder.

6. Click on the desired **file**. The file will be selected.

7. Click on **Open**. The Browse dialog box will close.

8. Click on the **Display As Icon check box**. The option will be selected.

9. Click on **OK**. The Insert Object dialog box will close.

Using OLE Objects

Object Linking and Embedding (OLE) allows you to launch another program from within Family Tree Maker. You might want to do this so you can open a word-processing file to display a detailed family story.

1. **Click** on **Picture/Object**. The Picture/Object menu will appear.

2. **Click** on **Insert Object**. The Insert Object dialog box will open.

3. **Click** on the **Create from File radio button**. The option will be selected.

TIP

If you click on the Create New radio button, you can select an object type from the list that appears. Then click on OK and the program will start.

4. **Click** on the **Browse button**. The Browse dialog box will open.

5. Use the **Look in drop-down menu** to select the desired folder.

6. Click on the desired **file**. The file will be selected.

7. Click on **Open**. The Browse dialog box will close.

8. Click on the **Display As Icon check box**. Family Tree Maker will insert an icon in the scrapbook.

9. Click on **OK**. The Insert Object dialog box will close.

Entering Information about Scrapbook Objects

To help you know what you have selected in your scrapbook, Family Tree Maker offers a More About screen for each scrapbook entry.

1. Click on the **More About button** for the selected scrapbook item. The More About Picture/Object dialog box will open.

2. Type a **caption** in the Caption field.

3. Type a **category** in the Category field.

TIP

Plan ahead before you use the Category field. Family Tree Maker allows you to categorize your scrapbook objects, making them easier to search.

4. Type a **description** for the object in the Description field.

5. Select the desired **Preferred check box(es)**. The option(s) will be selected.

TIP

Remember that while Family Tree Maker can display sound clips and OLE objects, you will only get the digitized images in a printed report.

---

6. Click on the **Include in show check box** if you want the object to display when you play the scrapbook.

7. Click on the **Include in printed Scrapbook check box** if you want the object to display in the printed scrapbook.

8. Click on **OK**. The More About Picture/Object dialog box will close.

Rearranging Scrapbook Objects

There might be a time when you want the items or objects in the scrapbook to display in a particular order that's different from the way you originally entered them.

Moving Objects

One way to rearrange the objects inserted in a scrapbook is to move them.

1. Click on the **object** you want to move. The object will be selected.

2. Click on **Edit**. The Edit menu will appear.

3. Click on **Cut Picture/Object**. The picture will be moved to the Clipboard.

4. Click in the **frame** where you want to place the object.

5. Click on **Edit**. The Edit menu will appear.

6. Click on **Paste Picture/ Object**. The object will be pasted in the new position.

Copying Objects

You can copy and paste a scrapbook item from the scrapbook of one individual to that of another.

1. Click on the **object** you want to copy.

2. Click on **Edit**. The Edit menu will appear.

3. Click on **Copy Picture/ Object**. The object will be copied to the Clipboard.

4. Click on the **Index of Individuals button**. The Index of Individuals dialog box will open.

5. Click on the **individual** into whose scrapbook you want to paste the object. The individual will be selected.

6. Click on **OK**. The new individual's scrapbook will open.

7. Click on the **frame** where you want to place the object.

8. Click on **Edit**. The Edit menu will appear.

9. Click on **Paste Picture/ Object**. The copied object will be placed in the scrapbook.

Editing Pictures and Objects

Family Tree Maker has included the ability to rotate, crop, mirror, and flip images.

1. Click on **Picture/Object**. The Picture/Object menu will appear.

2. Click on **Edit**. A message box will appear, encouraging you to use the original picture.

TIP

Family Tree Maker encourages you to edit the original file rather than a copy. If you click on Yes, the Insert Picture dialog box will open. If you click on No, the Edit Picture dialog box will open.

3. **Click and drag** the **mouse pointer** to highlight the area of the image you want to edit. The area will be selected.

4. **Click** on the **Crop button**. The picture will be cropped.

TIP

You can undo the changes by clicking on the Cancel button. The Edit Picture dialog box will close, and no changes will be made.

Searching for Objects

While it may not seem possible now, the more items you add, the quicker you will need to rely on the abilities of the Find features to locate specific scrapbook objects.

1. **Click** on **Edit**. The Edit menu will appear.

2. **Click** on **Find Picture/Object**. The Find Picture/Object dialog box will open.

NOTE

You must have the scrapbook open to use the Find Picture/Object menu command.

3. Click on the **Search down arrow**. The Search drop-down menu will appear.

4. Click on the **search option** you want to use. The option will be selected.

5. In the for field, **type** the **term** for which you want to search.

6. Click on the **Find next button**. The Family Page window will appear.

7. Click on the **Scrapbk button** for the individual who is in the Family Page. The individual's scrapbook will appear, and you will be able to view the scrapbook objects, one of which will fit your search criteria.

NOTE

Continue to click on the Find next button until the Family Tree Maker has found the individual you want. Once that person's Family Page is displayed, you can click on the Cancel button to close the Find Individual dialog box.

Sharing Your Scrapbook

When you have put together the digitized images with, say, the digitized interview of your relative, you will want to share it with others.

Playing a Scrapbook

Family reunions are a great place to share scrapbooks. If you have Family Tree Maker set up on a computer with speakers, there is no limit to what you can do.

1. Click on **Picture/Object**. The Picture/Object menu will appear.

2. Click on **Play Scrapbook**. The Play Scrapbook dialog box will open.

3. Use the **up and down arrows** in the Time between Pictures/Objects (in seconds) field to adjust the delay between objects.

4. Click on **OK**. The scrapbook will be played.

TIP

A sound file cannot play at the same time a slide is being viewed. If you have combined the two, you will find that you have a blank screen while the sound file runs its course.

Printing a Scrapbook

Most of the time, you will share your scrapbook by printing it out. Remember, the printed scrapbook includes only digitized images.

1. Click on **File**. The File menu will appear.

2. Click on **Print Preview**. The Scrapbook Print Preview window will open.

TIP

You can determine what will print in your scrapbook. Click on Contents, then click on Items to Include with each Picture/Object.

3. Click on the **Print button**. The Print Scrapbook Print Preview dialog box will open.

4a. Click on **OK**. The scrapbook will be printed.

OR

4b. Click on **Cancel**. The scrapbook will not be printed.

18

Creating a Family History Book

For many researchers, the ultimate goal is to publish a record of their ancestry. Family Tree Maker has long kept this in mind and offers one of the easiest ways to put a variety of reports together to share with family, friends, or colleagues. In this chapter, you'll learn how to:

- Select specific reports and trees
- Organize the selected items
- Work with images
- Add page breaks
- Create a customized index

Selecting Available Items

You have looked at many of the trees and reports that Family Tree Maker can create, but you might have been unaware that you can select these and put them together to create a book. One of the first things you have to do is decide what items to select. Following is a list of possible items to include in the book from the title page to the index, including lots of family trees and narrative reports.

- Front Matter (title page, copyright notice, and so on)
- Introduction
- Ancestor Trees
- Descendant Trees
- Hourglass Trees
- Kinship Reports
- Narrative Reports
- Timelines
- Calendars
- Bibliography
- Index

1. Click on the **Publishing Center button**. The Publishing Center will appear.

2. Click on **Create a Family Book**. The New Book dialog box will open.

3. Type the **book title** in the Book title field and **press** the **Tab key**. The cursor will move to the Author field.

4. Type the **author's name**.

5. Click on **OK**. The Books window will appear.

TIP

Another way to begin putting together a new book is to click on the Books menu. After the Books menu appears, click on New Book.

Selecting Front Matter

When you open any book, the first pages you look at contain what Family Tree Maker refers to as the front matter. The title page, copyright notice, dedication, and table of contents are such items. When you first create your book, you will need to decide which of these you want to include.

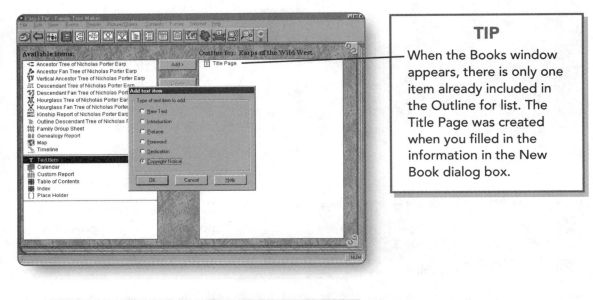

TIP

When the Books window appears, there is only one item already included in the Outline for list. The Title Page was created when you filled in the information in the New Book dialog box.

1. In the Available items list, **double-click** on **Text Item**. The Add text item dialog box will open.

2. Click on the desired **text item**. The item will be selected.

3. Click on **OK**. The selected text item will be added to the Outline for list.

4. In the Outline for list, **click** on the newly added **text item**. The option buttons will be activated.

5. Click on **Edit**. The text editor window will open and display the selected item.

6. Use the **toolbar buttons** to make changes to the item.

TIP

The text editor works much like any other word-processing program. If you click on one of the toolbar buttons, such as italics, before you type, then the text will be in italics. To change something that has already been typed, you must highlight the text before choosing one of the toolbar options.

7. Click on the **Close button**. When you are prompted to save the book item, click on OK.

NOTE

You are not limited to a single text item. You might want to repeat steps 1 through 6 to add additional items such as a dedication and an introduction.

Adding Trees and Reports

A book of your ancestors should contain a number of different trees and reports. It is important to keep your audience in mind when you're deciding what to include. You can create different books for different groups of individuals, so that the one you share with your family is more personal and less formal than the one you share with another genealogist.

1. **Click** on the **tree or report** you want to include. The tree or report will be highlighted.

2. **Click** on **Add**. The tree or report will be added to the Outline for list.

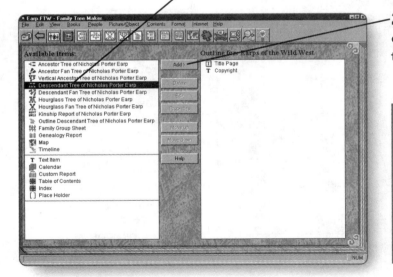

TIP

You can select any of the reports, trees, or other options in the Available items list. You will learn to organize them later in this chapter, in the "Organizing the Items" section.

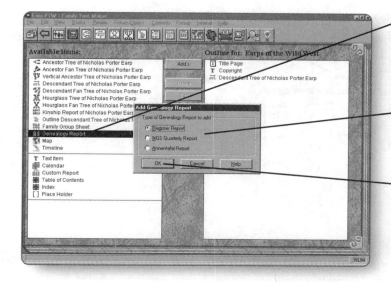

3. Double-click on **Genealogy Report** in the Available items list. The Add Genealogy Report dialog box will open.

4. Select the **type of Genealogy Report** to add. The option will be selected.

5. Click on **OK**. The Add Genealogy Report dialog box will close and the Genealogy Report will appear in the Outline for list.

Including Text with Pictures

Most of your family will want to see pictures in the book you share with them. While you can include them in some of the trees and reports, there are other times when you might want to have more control over the image. You can do so by adding a Text Item with Pictures.

1. In the Available Items list, **double-click** on **Text Item**. The Add text item dialog box will open.

2. Select the desired **text item**.

3. Click on **OK**. The Add text item dialog box will close.

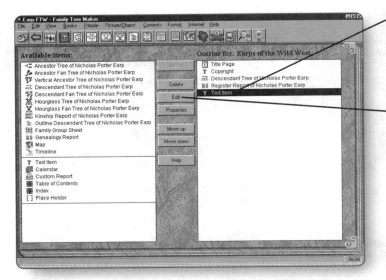

4. In the Outline for list, **click** on the newly added **text item**. Additional option buttons will be activated.

5. Click on **Edit**. The Text Item edit window will open.

6. Click on **Picture**. The Picture menu will appear.

7. Click on **Insert from Scrapbook**. The Individuals with Scrapbook Pictures dialog box will open.

8. Click on the **individual** whose scrapbook you want to access. The individual will be highlighted.

9. Click on **OK**. The Insert Scrapbook Picture dialog box will open.

NOTE

If the displayed individual's scrapbook does not include the picture you were expecting, you can click on Select new individual and the Individuals with Scrapbook Pictures dialog box will open again.

10. Click on the **picture** you want to include. The picture will be displayed in the Preview box, if you have the Preview Picture check box selected.

11. Click on **OK**. The Insert Scrapbook Picture dialog box will close and the picture will be included in the Text Item window.

12. **Type** the **text** you want to associate with the image.

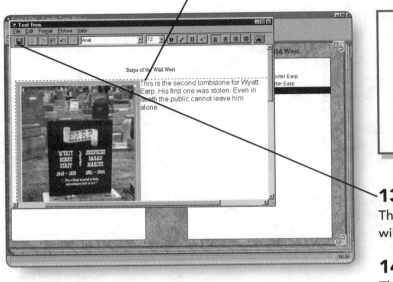

13. **Click** on the **Save button**. The changes to the text item will be saved.

14. **Click** on the **Close button**. The Text Item window will close.

Working with Outline Items

After you have decided which reports and trees you want to include in your book, you can begin to organize their order in the Outline for list. This is the order in which they will print when you send your book to the printer. You can also control which of your reports will start a new chapter in the book.

Organizing the Items

When you added to the Outline for list, Family Tree Maker simply placed the newly added tree or report at the bottom of the list. However, this might not be the order in which you want the items for the reports. You can add them in the order you want them to appear, or you can simply move them around after they are in the list.

1. In the Outline for list, **click** on the **tree or report** you want to move. The item will be highlighted.

2. Click on the **Move up or Move down button** to move the highlighted item.

NOTE

Although Family Tree Maker doesn't disable the buttons, you cannot move the Title Page. Family Tree Maker will tell you that the Title Page must be the first item in the book.

TIP

It is a good idea to have a plan before you start moving around the reports. For more information about publishing your family history with Family Tree Maker, and for some ideas about different types of family history book projects, you might want to read *Create Your Family History Book with Family Tree Maker Version 8: The Official Guide* (Prima Tech, 2000), by Marthe Arends.

Working with Item Properties

As you were putting your reports and trees into the order in which they now appear, you were probably visualizing the divisions of your book. If you look at any of the published family histories in your local genealogy library, you will see that they are broken into chapters to make using the book easier.

1. Click on the **report or tree** with which you want to work. The report or tree will be highlighted.

2. Click on the **Properties button**. The Item Properties dialog box will open.

3. Select the **This item begins a Chapter check box** if you want the item to be the first item in a new chapter. A check mark will appear in the check box.

4. Select the **Start this item on odd numbered page check box** if you want to control on what page this item will begin. A check mark will appear in the check box.

5. Click on **OK**. Your changes will be saved and the Item Properties dialog box will close.

TIP

You can use the Header/Footer options to determine which of your reports and trees will include header or footer information. The header is usually the title of the book. The footer is usually the page number.

Finalizing the Book

Family Tree Maker offers a few enhancements to help define your book and make it easier to read. After all, you want those who read the book to find it easy to use.

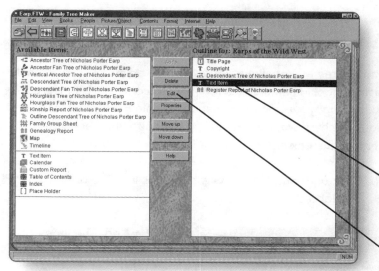

Adding Page Breaks

There might be times when you're working with one of the text items that you want to break up the text or put your images on separate pages. To do this, you will need to add a page break.

1. **Click** on the **text item** you want to edit. The text item will be highlighted.

2. **Click** on the **Edit button**. The Text Item window will appear.

3. **Click** on **Edit**. The Edit menu will appear.

4. **Click** on **Insert Page Break**. A new page will be added in the Text Item window.

5. **Click** on the **Close button**. Family Tree Maker will prompt you to save the changes, and the Text Item window will close.

TIP

You can undo the page break by putting the insertion point at the top of the page and pressing the Backspace key.

Creating a Customized Index

Family Tree Maker allows you to include an index in your family history book. Genealogists for years to come will be pleased to find that your book has an index. While Family Tree Maker does the hard work of organizing the page numbers, you control the look and feel of the index.

1. Click on **Index** in the Available items list. The option will be highlighted.

2. Click on **Add**. The index will be added to the end of the Outline for list.

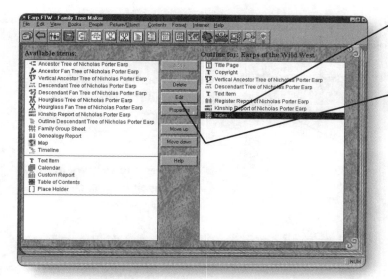

3. In the Outline for list, **click** on **Index**. The option will be highlighted.

4. Click on **Edit**. The Index of Individuals Report will appear.

5. Click on **Contents**. The Contents menu will appear.

6. Click on **Options**. The Options for Book Index dialog box will open.

7. Click on a **Columns radio button** to select the number of columns to include in the index. The option will be selected.

8. Click on the **Group first names under each surname check box**. A check mark will appear.

9. Click on the **Display index letters check box**. A check mark will appear.

10. Click on **OK**. Family Tree Maker will make the requested changes to the report.

TIP

You might want to view the index with all possible combinations of these choices to examine the effect each combination has on the ease of reading the index.

19

Creating Your Personal Family Tree Maker Home Page

While publishing a family history is still traditionally done by putting it on paper, the Internet has brought about a marvelous new way for people to publish their family histories. When publishing to paper, people tend to hold off publishing in an effort to get everything perfect. The Internet saves people from this need to delay, as they can always upload a revised version of their pages. In this chapter, you'll learn how to:

- Create your first home page
- Register your home page
- Add reports to your home page
- Add trees to your home page
- Remove items from your home page

Creating Your First Home Page

Computers can intimidate genealogists, and many genealogists consider the Internet to be the biggest computer of them all—though it is not really a single computer. So, it is understandable that you might be hesitant when thinking about creating a family history Web page.

Working with the Wizard

Family Tree Maker is following the lead of many other software programs by adding wizards to help you perform certain tasks. The Family Home Page wizard walks you through putting together a basic home page.

1. Click on the **Publishing Center button**. The Publishing Center will appear.

2. Click on **Create a Family Home Page**. The Family Home Page wizard will appear.

NOTE

The Family Home Page wizard helps you learn how to create a family history home page on the Family Tree Maker Web site.

3. Click on the **Next button**. The wizard will begin to ask you questions.

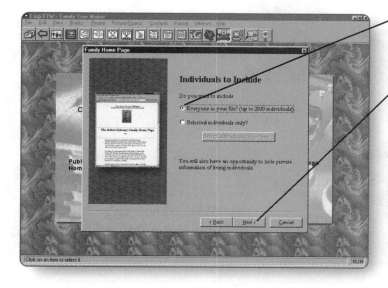

4. Answer the **question** asked. The wizard will record the answer.

5. Click on **Next**. The wizard will ask the next question.

6. Continue to answer the wizard's **questions**. When it has asked all the questions, the wizard will tell you it's time to go online.

NOTE

You might need to go online to register before you create your home page. If so, see the following section, "Registering Your Home Page," and then return and rerun the wizard so that it can upload your page to your site.

Registering Your Home Page

The wizard has put together a general page for you to upload. Since this is the first Web page you have created, you will need to register with the Family Tree Maker site before the page can be uploaded.

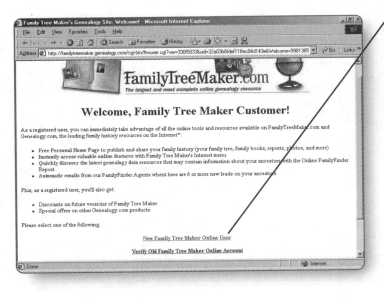

1. Click on the **Family Tree Maker Online button**. Your browser will open.

2. Use the **scroll bar** to scroll to the bottom of the Web page and **click** on **New Family Tree Maker Online User**. The Family Tree Maker Online Sign-Up screen will appear.

3. Type your **first name** in the First Name field and **press** the **Tab key**. The cursor will move to the next field.

4. Supply the requested **information** for the rest of the form and **click** on the **Submit button** at the bottom of the page. Your registration will be sent and you will be able to begin adding items to your home page.

Working with Your Home Page

After the wizard has helped you upload your first Web page, you can enhance it by adding additional reports, an InterneTree, or even a book. The beauty of your home page is that you can change what is available whenever you wish. Most of the reports that you can print to paper can be used on the Family Tree Maker site as well.

Adding Reports

Adding reports to your home page will make them viewable to anyone who visits your Web page. These reports will be added to the indexing and searching functions found on Family Tree Maker's Web site and to the Genealogy.com search page. There are many reports and trees that you can publish to your family home page, including:

- Outline Descendant Trees
- Custom Reports
- Genealogy Reports (Register, NGSQ, or Ahnentafel)
- Family Tree Maker Books

1. Click on the **report button** for the tree or report you want to add to your home page. The report will appear.

2. Click on **Internet**. The Internet menu will appear.

3. Click on **Publish Report to the Internet**. Family Tree Maker will display a message box, letting you know that it is preparing the report for publication to your home page. It will then begin to upload the report, keeping you informed of its progress. After the information has been uploaded, you can have Family Tree Maker take you to your home page.

TIP

While Family Tree Maker is uploading the report, it will also ask you if you want to contribute your Family File to the World Family Tree. The World Family Tree is a collection of CD-ROMs with Family Files from other researchers. You can answer Yes to contribute or No if you do not want to contribute your Family File to the World Family Tree.

4. Click on the **Publishing Center button**. The Publishing Center will appear.

5. Click on **View your Home Page**. Your browser will appear.

6. Use the **scroll bar** to scan through your Web page.

NOTE

You will see that in addition to working in the Family Tree Maker program, you can also upload other items to your home page, including pictures and Web links. Click on the Add to or Edit This Section link to customize your home page.

Adding an InterneTree

An InterneTree is a box-style tree. However, unlike the normal box-style reports, this one is interactive. Visitors to your home page can use an index and move through the generations. For each person in the tree, they will see the name, birth date, and death date for the individual.

NOTE

You must be in the Family Page before you can add your InterneTree.

---

1. Click on **Internet**. The Internet menu will appear.

2. Click on **Publish Family Tree to the Internet**. Family Tree Maker will remind you that you need to be connected to the Internet.

3. Click on **OK**. The Include dialog box will open.

4. Select the **individuals** you want to include. The radio button will reflect your choice.

NOTE

NOTE

If you choose Selected individuals, you will need to click on the Individuals to Include button to select the specific individuals you want to include.

5. Click on **OK**. The InterneTree information will be uploaded to your home page.

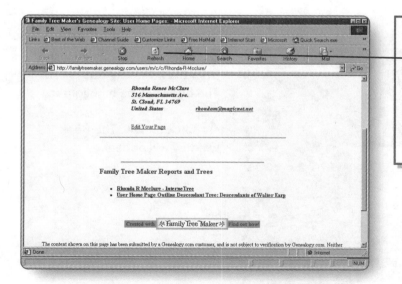

NOTE

You might need to click on the Refresh button in your browser to see the InterneTree in the list of reports on your home page.

Adding a Book

Just as you can print your family history book to paper and publish it to send to your family and fellow researchers, you can also include it on your home page. This offers you the chance to publish your book while it's still a work in progress. As you find new information or correct inaccurate conclusions, you can simply upload a new version of the book to your home page.

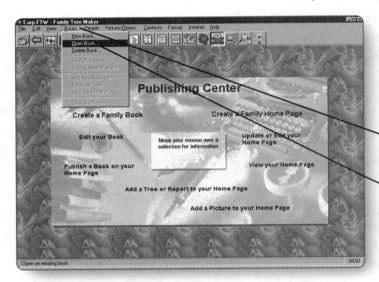

1. Click on **Books**. The Books menu will appear.

2. Click on **Open Book**. The Open Book dialog box will open.

3. Select the **book** you want from the Available books list. The book will be highlighted.

4. Click on **OK**. The Book window will appear.

5. Click on **Internet**. The Internet menu will appear.

6. Click on **Publish Book to the Internet**. Family Tree Maker will upload the book, as it has already been designed, to your home page.

Removing Items from Your Home Page

Don't think that just because Family Tree Maker has uploaded these pages, you have no control over whether they remain on the home page. You determine what stays.

Removing a Family Tree Maker Report or Book

Removing a report or book that you have placed on your home page is not done through the Family Tree Maker program. It is done at the Family Tree Maker Web site—specifically, at your home page.

1. Click on **Edit Your Page**. Your browser will take you to the new page.

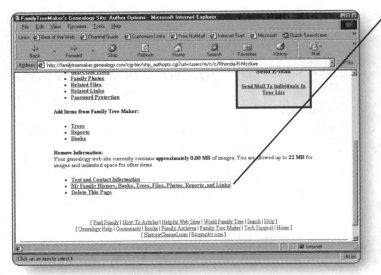

2. Scroll to the **Remove Information section** at the bottom of the edit page and **click** on the **link** for the information you want to remove. The Removing page will appear.

3. Click on the **check box** next to the item you wish to remove. A check mark will appear.

4. Click on the **Remove Selected Items button**. The item(s) will be removed.

Deleting Your Home Page

You are not limited to removing specific items from your home page. You can also delete the entire home page if you need to—you can always re-create it at a later date.

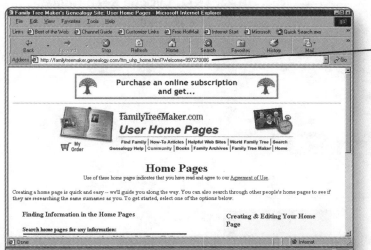

1. Open your **browser.**

2. Type **http://www.familytreemaker. com/ftm_uhp_home.html** and **press Enter.** The Family Tree Maker User Home Pages site will appear.

3. Scroll to the **bottom** of the page and **click** on **Delete your home page.** The Delete Your Home Page screen will appear.

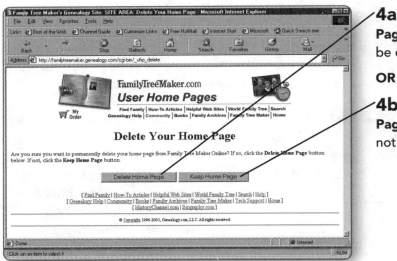

4a. Click on **Delete Home Page**. Your home page will be deleted.

OR

4b. Click on **Keep Home Page**. Your home page will not be deleted.

CAUTION

If you elect to delete your home page, all the reports and trees that were available on your home page will no longer show up online.

Part V Review Questions

1. In Family Tree Maker, what is a scrapbook? *See "Using the Scrapbook" in Chapter 17*

2. What are the three different types of objects you can include in the scrapbook? *See "Inserting Scrapbook Objects" in Chapter 17*

3. How can you rearrange the order of your scrapbook objects? *See "Rearranging Scrapbook Objects" in Chapter 17*

4. What reports can you include in a family history book? *See "Selecting Available Items" in Chapter 18*

5. How can you add a tree or report to your family history book? *See "Adding Trees and Reports" in Chapter 18*

6. How do you include pictures in your family history book? *See "Including Text with Pictures" in Chapter 18*

7. What are the ways you can customize the index to your family history book? *See "Creating a Customized Index" in Chapter 18*

8. What types of reports can you include on your family history home page? *See "Working with Your Home Page" in Chapter 19*

9. How can you add a family history book to your home page? *See "Adding a Book" in Chapter 19*

10. How can you remove a report or book from your home page? *See "Removing a Family Tree Maker Report or Book" in Chapter 19*

PART VI

Advanced Family Tree Maker Methods

20

Working with Marriage Facts and Custom Fact Names

Working with the Marriage field in the Family Page might overshadow some of the other features you have used in the More About Marriage Facts window. Custom facts offer you an unlimited number of life events, though as your experience with the program grows, you might want to do away with some of the facts you have created. In this chapter, you'll learn how to:

- Work with the marriage fact
- Enter alternate marriage events
- Coordinate the Marriage Fact and More About Marriage Facts options
- Remove a previously created custom fact name

Working with the Marriage Fact in the Family Page

It is almost second nature, as a genealogist, to want to enter a date of marriage for the parents of a family. Understanding how Family Tree Maker works with the information submitted here will prevent frustration when you are generating reports.

It is extremely tempting to fill in a date in the Marriage date field on the Family Page, even when you don't have one. The Marriage date field should be reserved for those times when you have an actual marriage date, for instance when you have in your possession (or when you have seen) a marriage license or certificate.

TIP

Instead of putting an estimated date in the Marriage date field, take advantage of the More About Marriage Facts options. See the "Using More About Marriage Facts" section later in this chapter.

Understanding Beginning Status

The Beginning status field can be ignored if you wish. If you are not entering information into the Marriage date field, the Beginning status field might help you remember what you know about that couple's relationship.

1. Click on the **Beginning status down arrow**. The Beginning status drop-down menu will appear.

TIP

If you hold the mouse pointer over the Beginning status field, a pop-up Help message will appear, explaining the purpose of this option in Family Tree Maker.

2. Click on the **appropriate status**. The status will be selected.

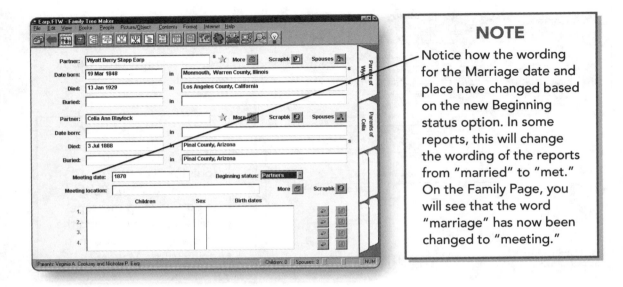

NOTE

Notice how the wording for the Marriage date and place have changed based on the new Beginning status option. In some reports, this will change the wording of the reports from "married" to "met." On the Family Page, you will see that the word "marriage" has now been changed to "meeting."

Using More About Marriage Facts

While you were introduced to the More About Marriage Facts window earlier, the focus then was on the ending of the marriage. Actually, the More About Marriage Facts window can be used in conjunction with or instead of the Marriage date field.

1. Click on the **More button**. The More About Marriage Facts window will appear.

2. Click on the **Fact down arrow**. The Fact drop-down menu will appear.

3. Click on the **appropriate fact** from the list. The fact will be selected.

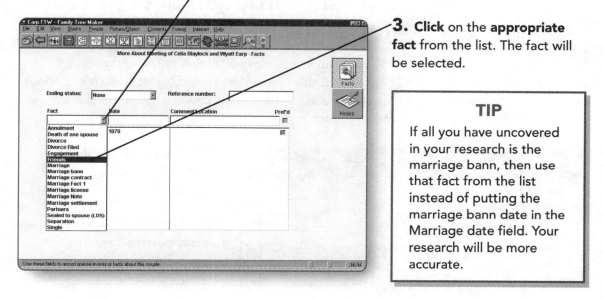

> ### TIP
>
> If all you have uncovered in your research is the marriage bann, then use that fact from the list instead of putting the marriage bann date in the Marriage date field. Your research will be more accurate.

4. Press the **Tab key**. The cursor will move to the Date field.

5. Type the **date of the event** and **press** the **Tab key**. The cursor will move to the Comment/Location field.

6. Type the **location** and **press** the **Tab key**. The new event will be saved.

Getting Family Page and More About Marriage Facts to Work Together

You will want to pay close attention to the options in the Beginning status menu. When selecting from the More About Marriage Facts menu, you will need to select a preferred marriage fact.

1. Click on the **Family Page button**. The Family Page will appear.

2. Click on the **Beginning status down arrow**. The Beginning status drop-down menu will appear.

3. Select the **Married** option from the list. The option will be selected.

NOTE

Be sure that the Marriage date and Marriage location fields are empty on the Family Page.

4. **Type** the **marriage date and place**. Make note of the date and place.

5. **Click** on the **More button**. The More About Marriage window will appear.

6. **Click** on the **Fact down arrow**. The Fact drop-down menu will appear.

7. **Click** on **Partners**. The Partners fact will be selected.

8. **Press** the **Tab key**. The cursor will move to the Date field.

9. Type the **date** and **press** the **Tab key.** The cursor will move to Comment/Location field.

TIP

Be sure that the date in question is different than the marriage date entered in Step 4.

10. Type the **place or comment** and **press** the **Tab key**. The cursor will disappear.

11. Click on the **Pref'd check box**. A check mark will appear.

12. Press the **Tab key**. The new marriage fact will be placed in the event list.

13. Click on the **Family Page button**.

The Family Page will appear. Notice that the Family Page has changed. The Marriage date and location fields have been renamed Meeting date and Meeting location. The date information reflects the new date entered. Also, notice that the Beginning status field reflects the Partners selection.

Removing a Custom Fact Name

One of the questions Family Tree Maker users often ask pertains to custom facts that they create and then want to delete.

Verifying That No One is Using the Fact

Before you can do anything with the custom fact name in your Fact list, you must first verify that no one in the database is still linked to the fact.

1. Click on the **Report button**. The Report window will open.

2. Click on the **Format button**. The Report Format dialog box will open.

3. Click on **Custom Report**. The Custom Report will be selected.

4. Click on **OK**. The Report Format dialog box will close.

5. Click on the **Individuals to Include button**. The Include dialog box will open.

6. Click on the **Selected individuals radio button**. The option will be selected.

7. Click on the **Individuals to Include button**. The Individuals to Include dialog box will open.

TIP

If there are individuals in the You have included these individuals list, click on the button to remove them from the list.

8. **Click** on the **Find button**. The Add Individuals dialog box will open.

9. **Click** on the **Search down arrow**. The Search drop-down menu will appear.

10. **Select** the **fact** you wish to remove. The fact will be selected.

11. **Press** the **Tab key**. The cursor will move to the for field.

12. Type **!=**.

NOTE

By entering the characters != you are telling Family Tree Maker to show you anyone with anything in that field. This is the best way to find anyone still associated with the fact.

13. **Click** on **OK**. The Add Individuals dialog box will close.

14. **Click** on **OK**. The Individuals to Include dialog box will close.

15. Double-click on **one of the names** that appears in the report. The Individual Facts Card will open.

16. Click on the **fact**. The fact will be highlighted.

17. Press the **Delete key.** The fact will be removed from the list of facts for that individual.

18. Click on **OK.** The Individual Facts Card will close.

TIP

You need to repeat steps 15 through 18 for each person who appeared on the Custom Report.

Think Rename, Not Delete

Once there is no longer anyone using the fact, you can get rid of it. You won't actually be deleting the fact; instead, you'll be renaming it. Before beginning this section, be sure you are in the More About Facts window for anyone in your database.

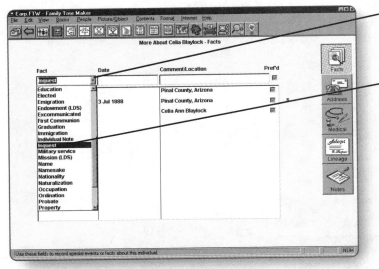

1. **Click** on the **Fact down arrow**. The Fact drop-down menu will appear.

2. **Select** the **fact to be removed** and **press** the **Tab key**. The fact will be selected and the cursor will move to the Date field.

3. **Type** a **date** and **press** the **Tab key** twice. The fact will be added to the More About Facts window.

NOTE

In order for Family Tree Maker to recognize the fact, you must enter either a date or a place. Hitting the Tab key three times will not allow you to add an empty fact to the list. The fact must be added to the list before you can change its name.

4. **Highlight** the **name** of the fact to be deleted. That fact name will be selected.

5. **Type** the **name** of one of the unused facts in the Fact list. The name of the fact will change.

> ### TIP
>
> The Family Tree Maker KnowledgeBase at Genealogy.com suggests changing a fact to be deleted to the Caste event, as this is not often used in your general research.

6. **Press** the **Tab key**. The Change Fact Name message box will appear.

7a. **Click** on **Yes**. The fact name will be changed.

OR

7b. **Click** on **No**. The fact name will not be changed.

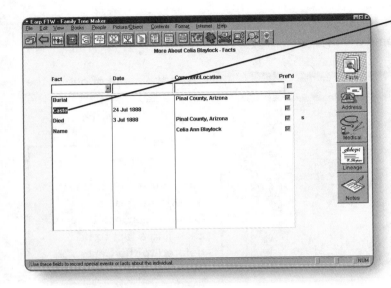

8. Click on the **newly named fact**. The fact will be highlighted.

9. Press the **Delete key**. The fact name will be deleted.

10. Press the **Tab key**. The fact will be removed from the individual's list of facts.

21

Working with GEDCOM Files and Other Family Files

At some point in your research, it is possible that you will get a database from another researcher or you will want to share your database with someone. Such sharing is usually done through GEDCOM files. There will also be times when you will want to keep some of your research in a separate Family File. In this chapter, you'll learn how to:

- Export a complete Family File using GEDCOM
- Export a partial Family File using GEDCOM
- Import a GEDCOM file to an existing Family File
- Create a new Family File

Creating a GEDCOM File

When it comes time to share with other researchers, the easiest way to share your information is through a GEDCOM file. This allows researchers to import your work regardless of whether or not they are using Family Tree Maker.

Sharing Your Complete Family File

When sharing with others in your immediate family, you will probably want to share your entire database.

1. **Click** on the **Family Page button**. The Family Page will appear.

2. **Click** on **File**. The File menu will appear.

3. **Click** on **Copy/Export Family File**. The New Family File dialog box will open.

NOTE

While Family Tree Maker allows you to add digitized images, sounds, and objects, these links are not supported by GEDCOM. If you share a GEDCOM file, these items will not be included in the GEDCOM file.

4. Click on the **Save as type down arrow**. The Save as type menu will appear.

5. Click on **GEDCOM (*.GED)**. The GEDCOM option will be selected.

NOTE

Family Tree Maker automatically names the GEDCOM file with the same name you originally gave the Family File. You can double-click on this name to highlight it and type a new name if you want.

TIP

Pay attention to where Family Tree Maker is saving the file so you can find it later when you want to share it.

6. Click on the **Save button**. The Export to GEDCOM dialog box will open.

NOTE

Generally the default settings will work when sharing a GEDCOM file. However, if you are a Latter-Day Saint creating a file for TempleReady, you will want to use the Destination drop-down menu to select TempleReady.

7. Click on **OK**. The Export to GEDCOM dialog box will close and the file will be saved.

Sharing Part of a Family File

Usually when you are sharing with individuals you have met through a genealogical society or on the Internet, you will only want to send them the line that you share in common.

TIP

To determine the individual to select, first you need to determine the line you want to share. Find the child of that line in the Index of Individuals.

1. Press the **F2 key**. The Index of Individuals dialog box will open.

2. Click on the **appropriate individual**. He or she will be selected.

3. Click on **OK**. The Index of Individuals dialog box will close.

4. Click on the **Parents of tab** for the spouse of the selected individual. The Family Page will display the new family.

5. Click on the **spouse as a child.** The child will be highlighted.

6. Click on **People.** The People menu will appear.

7. Move the **mouse pointer** to Fix Relationship Mistakes. The Fix Relationship Mistakes menu will appear.

8. Click on **Detach Child.** The child will be detached from his or her parents.

NOTE

For a refresher on how to detach a child, see Chapter 12, "Fixing Relationships and Duplicates." In this case, you are temporarily detaching the child. You do not want to detach the siblings.

9. Use the **Index of Individuals** to relocate the individual selected in Step 2.

10. Click on the **All-in-One Tree button**. The All-in-One Tree will open.

11. Click on the **Options button**. The Options for All-in-One Tree dialog box will open.

TIP

While this example is using the All-in-One Tree to isolate the desired individuals, you can also create a list of individuals using the Custom Report. For detailed information on searching for individuals to include in the Custom Report, see Chapter 22, "Working with Custom Reports and Research Journal Features."

12. Click on the **Show unconnected step-family trees check box**. The option will be selected.

13. Click on **OK**. The Options for All-in-One Tree dialog box will close.

14. Click on **File**. The File menu will appear.

15. Click on **Copy/Export Individuals in Tree**. The Copy/Export Individuals in All-in-One Tree dialog box will open.

NOTE

At this point, you can select the GEDCOM option from the Save as type drop-down menu and name the file, as you did earlier in the "Sharing Your Complete Family File" section.

Importing a GEDCOM File

Just as you will share GEDCOM files, you will also receive them. You can import a GEDCOM file directly into your Family File. However, this must be done from the Family Page.

TIP

Before beginning this process, it is a good idea to save your Family File as a backup, either by copying it elsewhere on your hard drive or by selecting Backup Family File from the File menu.

---

1. Click on **File**. The File menu will appear.

2. Click on **Append/Merge Family File**. The Append Family File dialog box will open.

NOTE

Before you add someone's GEDCOM file to your Family File, it is a good idea to first create a new Family File of the data. This allows you to evaluate the data before it gets mixed into your own Family File. Once you have determined the data's accuracy, you can then follow the steps in this section to add it to your personal Family File. To see how to create a new Family File with a GEDCOM file, see the "Opening a GEDCOM File as a New Family File" section later in this chapter.

3. Click on the **Files of type down arrow**. The Files of type drop-down menu will appear.

4. Click on **GEDCOM (*.GED)**. The GEDCOM file type will be selected.

TIP

These same steps can be used to append someone else's Family File or another one you have created. Instead of selecting GEDCOM (*.GED) from the Files of type menu, you would select Family Tree Maker for Windows (*.FTW).

5. Click on the **appropriate GEDCOM file**. The file will be selected.

6. Click on the **Append file button**. A warning message will appear.

7. Click on **OK**. The warning message will close and the Import from GEDCOM dialog box will open.

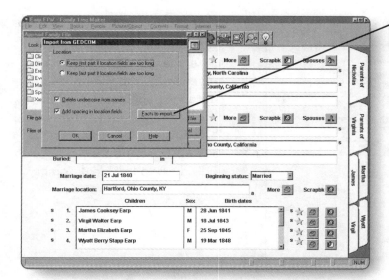

8. Click on the **Facts to import button**. The Facts to Import dialog box will open.

NOTE

It is a good idea to look and see where Family Tree Maker wants to put some of the facts that will be imported. This is even more important when the GEDCOM file you are importing is coming from someone who is not using Family Tree Maker.

9. Click on **OK**. The Facts to Import dialog box will close.

10. **Click** on **OK**. The Import from GEDCOM dialog box will close, the GEDCOM file will be appended to the Family File, and a message box will open.

11. **Click** on **OK**. The message box will close and the Individuals to Include dialog box will open.

NOTE

This dialog box is the same as the one you were introduced to in Chapter 10, "Searching Your Family Tree File." Usually you will select everyone in the GEDCOM file using the ⟩⟩ button.

12. **Click** on **OK**. The Append File dialog box will open.

13a. Click on **Display merge report**. The Merge Individual Report will open.

OR

13b. Click on **Merge matching information**. The Merge Individuals dialog box will open.

OR

13c. Click on **Append only (no merge)**. The Append File dialog box will close and the individuals will be added to your database.

TIP

If you need a refresher on how to check the Family File for duplicates, see Chapter 12, "Fixing Relationships and Duplicates."

Opening a Different Family File

As your research progresses, it is conceivable that you might have more than one Family File. You might decide to create a Family File for a single-surname study or to keep a record of all those individuals to whom you haven't been able to figure out a connection.

Using the Open Family File Option

When you open a different Family File, you are actually doing two things. As you tell Family Tree Maker to open the other Family File, Family Tree Maker also closes the already open Family File.

1. Click on **File**. The File menu will appear.

2. Click on **Open Family File**. The Open Family File dialog box will open.

TIP

You can also open the Open Family File dialog box by pressing Ctrl+O.

---

3. Click on the **Family File** you want to open. The file will be selected.

4. Click on the **Open button**. The Family File will open.

NOTE

The Append file button in the Open Family File dialog box allows you to append another Family File to the last Family File you had open. It works much the same as appending a GEDCOM file, discussed earlier in this chapter.

TIP

There are times when Family Tree Maker will question whether you are a member of the Family File. It might also ask you if you want to run a FamilyFinder report. If you would like to run a FamilyFinder report, click on Yes and Family Tree Maker will run the report from the Internet. For more information, see Chapter 10 "Searching Your Family Tree File."

Using File History

Family Tree Maker will remember the last four Family Files you worked with, including the currently open Family File. You can access this history list to return to a previous Family File.

1. Click on **File**. The File menu will appear.

2. Click on the **desired Family File**. That Family File will replace the currently open Family File.

Opening a GEDCOM File as a New Family File

In addition to appending a GEDCOM file to an existing Family File, you can also create a new Family File using a GEDCOM file as the source of the data.

1. Click on **File**. The File menu will appear.

2. Click on **Open Family File**. The Open Family File dialog box will open.

3. Click on the **Files of type down arrow**. The Files of type menu will appear.

4. Click on **GEDCOM (*.GED)**. The GEDCOM file type will be selected.

NOTE

If you have not saved your Family Files in the default Family Tree Maker directory, you might need to use the Look in drop-down menu to select the appropriate folder on your system where the Family File is stored.

5. Click on the **appropriate GEDCOM file**. The file will be selected.

6. Click on the **Open button**. The New Family File dialog box will open.

7. Type the **name** of the new Family File.

8. Click on the **Save button**. The Import from GEDCOM dialog box will open.

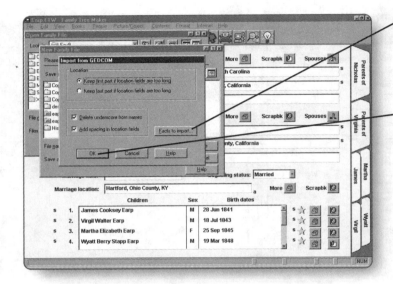

9a. **Click** on the **Facts to import button**. The Facts to Import dialog box will open.

OR

9b. **Click** on **OK**. A message box will appear, telling you that the import is complete.

10. If you followed Step 9b, **click** on **OK** to close the message box and go into the new Family File.

22

Working with Custom Reports and Research Journal Features

As your research progresses, you will find that the number of individuals in your Family File prevents you from knowing each one personally. The Custom Report allows you to generate a report of selected individuals, geared toward the research you need to do at the time. When coupled with the Research Journal to plot and track your research progress, you have a powerful tool. In this chapter, you'll learn how to:

- Use Custom Reports to select individuals based on a common name, date, or location
- Remove individuals from the Custom Report
- Track your research in the Research Journal
- Work with the Research Journal's categories

Using the Find Button to Include Individuals in the Custom Report

The Custom Report is a robust tool to use when planning a research trip to a county courthouse or localized regional facility. With the search functions of the Custom Report, you can create a report of just those individuals who fit your research criteria.

1. **Click** on the **Report button**. The Report window will open.

2. **Click** on the **Format button**. The Report Format dialog box will open.

3. **Click** on **Custom Report**. The Custom Report will be selected.

4. **Click** on **OK**. The Report Format dialog box will close.

Searching by Name

There will be times when your research is in a manuscript collection or other compilation devoted to a given family name. Compiling a list of those individuals in your database helps to ensure that as you research in these records, you do not overlook anyone presently included in your Family File.

1. **Click** on the **Individuals to Include button**. The Include dialog box will open.

NOTE

The Custom Report will reveal the list of the last individuals selected. This could be all of the individuals in your Family File or it could be a selected group. The individuals included in the current report are displayed along the bottom of the Family Tree Maker window.

2. **Click** on the **Individuals to Include button**. The Individuals to Include dialog box will open.

3. **Click** on the **Find button**. The Add Individuals dialog box will open.

TIP

Because the report's list of individuals is cumulative, if there is anyone in the You have included these individuals list, you will want to remove them before opening the Add Individuals dialog box. You can remove them by clicking on the ≪ button.

4. Click on the **Search down arrow**. The Search drop-down menu will appear.

5. Click on **Name**. The Name search will be selected.

6. Press the **Tab key**. The cursor will move to the for field.

7. Type the **surname** you want to find.

8. Click on **OK**. The You have included these individuals list will be updated.

9. Click on **OK**. The Custom Report will be modified.

Searching by Date

There will be times when the records you are using will be date sensitive. Searching for specific dates in your Family File will seclude those individuals in the Custom Report, ensuring that you don't overlook anyone.

1. Click on the **Individuals to Include button**. The Include dialog box will open.

2. Click on the **Individuals to Include button**. The Individuals to Include dialog box will open.

3. Click on the [«] **button**. Everyone from the You have included these individuals list will be removed.

4. Click on the **Find button**. The Add Individuals dialog box will open.

5. Click on the **Search down arrow**. The Search drop-down menu will appear.

6. Click on the **selected date**. That event date will be selected.

7. Press the **Tab key**. The cursor will move to the for field.

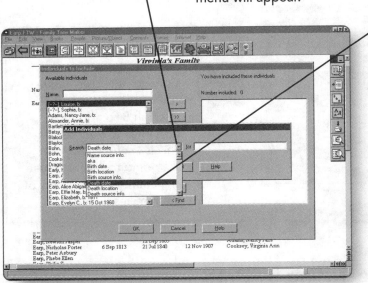

TIP

To create a blanket search of all date fields, select Any and all date fields from the Search menu. This will tell Family Tree Maker to search all fact dates in your Family File.

8. Type the **date** for which you want to search.

9. Click on **OK**. The You have included these individuals list will be updated.

The following table shows you the many ways you can search for dates in your Family File.

If you type this	Family Tree Maker will find this
<10/2/1988, or BEFORE 10/2/1988, or BEF 10/2/1988	All dates before October 2, 1988, including dates entered as "Before October 2, 1988"
<=10/2/1988	The date October 2, 1988 and all dates before it, including dates entered as "Before October 2, 1988"
>10/2/1988, or AFTER 10/2/1988, or AFT 10/2/1988	All dates after October 2, 1988, including dates entered as "After October 2, 1988"
>=10/2/1988	The date October 2, 1988 and all dates after it, including dates entered as "After October 2, 1988"
ABOUT 10/2/1988, or CIRCA 10/2/1988, or EST 10/2/1988	All dates entered as "About October 2,1988," "Circa October 2, 1988," or "Est October 2, 1988"
10/2/1988..10/2/1990, or >=10/2/1988..<=10/2/1990	All dates between October 2, 1988 and October 2, 1990, including those two days
>10/2/1988..<10/2/1990	All dates between October 2, 1988 and October 2, 1990, not including those two days
UNKNOWN or ?	All dates entered as "Unknown" or "?"

Searching by Location

When you incorporate the location search in your Custom Report, you create an effective research tool for working with the records. Knowing who was born or married, who died, or who was living in a locality you will be researching ensures that you will have a list of all individuals with you. That way, you will not have to wonder whether you overlooked someone.

1. Click on the **Individuals to Include button**. The Include dialog box will open.

2. Click on the **Individuals to Include button**. The Individuals to Include dialog box will open.

3. Click on the **≪ button**. Everyone from the You have included these individuals list will be removed.

4. Click on the **Find button**. The Add Individuals dialog box will open.

5. Click on the **Search down arrow**. The Search menu will appear.

6. Click on the **selected event location**. That event location will be selected.

7. Press the **Tab key**. The cursor will move to the for field.

8. Type the **location** for which you want to search.

TIP

To generate a Custom Report of individuals who were born, married, and died in a given locality, you will need to follow steps 4 through 9 three times, selecting Birth location, Marriage location, and then Death location from the Search drop-down menu.

9. Click on **OK**. The You have included these individuals list will be updated.

Searching by Relationship

Using the relationship search in the Custom Report is an excellent way to create a report of individuals that can then be saved to a GEDCOM file or a new Family File.

1. Click on the **Individuals to Include button**. The Include dialog box will open.

2. Click on the **Individuals to Include button**. The Individuals to Include dialog box will open.

3. Click on the ◄◄ **button**. Everyone from the You have included these individuals list will be removed.

4. Click on the **selected individual** in the Available individuals list. The individual will be selected.

5. Click on the **Find button**. The Add Individuals dialog box will open.

6. Click on the **Search down arrow**. The Search drop-down menu will appear.

7. Click on the **selected relationship**. The relationship will be selected.

8. Click on **OK**. The You have included these individuals list will be updated.

TIP

Two of the available relationship searches can be accomplished using the Ancestors or Descendants buttons. However, if you want to generate a search of descendants of an individual that does not include spouses, you will need to use the option found in the Add Individuals dialog box (accessed by clicking on the Find button).

NOTE

You can combine any or all of these different searches to come up with the exact group of individuals you want in your Custom Report. First decide what your goal is and then figure out which of the many search options will help you fulfill that goal. Don't get discouraged if you have to try different approaches to the search. You will get it eventually.

Using the Find Button to Remove Individuals

After you have created a list of individuals using the myriad searches available, you might discover that you want to remove selected individuals from the list, especially if you are trying to create a report of individuals from which to generate a new Family File or GEDCOM file.

1. Click on an **individual** in the You have included these individuals list. The individual will be selected.

2. Click on the **Find button**. The Remove Individuals dialog box will open.

3. Click on the **Search down arrow**. The Search drop-down menu will appear.

4. Click on the desired **search option**. The option will be selected.

NOTE

You have the same search options in the Find and Remove search as you had in the Find and Include search. It just works in reverse, removing those individuals who fit the search criteria.

5. Press the **Tab key**. The cursor will move to the for field.

6. Type the **text, date, or name** for which you want to search.

7. Click on **OK**. The You have included these individuals list will be updated.

TIP

Once you have the You have included these individuals list to your liking, click on OK in the Individuals to Include dialog box to close it. The Custom Report will then be updated.

Formatting Your Custom Report

Once you have finally selected the individuals for your Custom Report, you will want to take as much care in the design of the report. You want to make sure it has enough information to easily identify the individuals included on the report.

1. Click on **Items to Include**. The Items to Include in Report dialog box will open.

2. Click on the ⟪ **button**. The Each row of your report will contain list will be erased.

3. Click on an **item** in the Available items list. The item will be selected.

4. Click on the **inclusion button**. The Options dialog box will open.

NOTE

For most of the items, the Options dialog box will simply question whether you want to include only preferred dates.

5. **Click** on the **Format down arrow**. The Format drop-down menu will appear.

6. **Click** on the **appropriate format**. The format will be selected

NOTE

As you make your choices, the sample in the lower-left corner of the dialog box will change.

7. **Click** on **OK**. The Options dialog box will close and the item will be listed in the Each row of your report will contain list.

TIP

Your report will probably need to contain the name of the individuals, at least one date (for identification purposes), and perhaps the name of the spouse (to make it easier to search for females during your research).

Saving as a New Family File or GEDCOM File

Once you have created the Custom Report that you want, you might want to create a new Family File or GEDCOM file of those individuals.

TIP

Be sure you have your Custom Report open and that it contains just the people you want to include in the new file. Only those individuals who appear on the Custom Report will be included in the new file.

1. Click on **File**. The File menu will appear.

2. Click on **Copy/Export Individuals in Report**. The Copy/Export Individuals in Report dialog box will open.

3. Type the **name** of the new file.

4. Select the appropriate **option** from the Save as type drop-down menu. The option will be selected.

5. Click on the **Save button**.

NOTE

If you are creating a new Family File, Family Tree Maker will begin to export the individuals' information into the file. If you are creating a GEDCOM file, refer to Chapter 21, "Working with GEDCOM Files and Other Family Files" for more information.

Taking Advantage of Research Journal Features

Many people think that the Research Journal must remain in the format shown when you first begin to use it. However, by taking advantage of the Research Journal options, you can tailor the report to include only what you want to see.

Selecting Items Marked as Done or Not Done

The Research Journal is your road map of the research you have done and the research that still must be accomplished. There will be times when you will want to see it all, and other times when you will want to see only what you have done or what is left to do.

1. Click on the **FamilyFinder Center button**. The FamilyFinder Center will open.

2. Click on the **My Research Journal/To-Do List**. The Research Journal will open.

3. Click on the **Items to Display button**. The Items to Display in Research Journal dialog box will open.

4. Select a **Show items marked option**. The option will be selected.

5. Click on **OK**. The Items to Display in Research Journal dialog box will close.

The Research Journal will reflect the changes to the items listed based on whether the To-Do item has been done or is still pending.

Selecting To-Do Categories

Another way to affect the format of the Research Journal is through the To-Do categories. Usually based on resources or repositories, the To-Do categories allow you to narrow the focus of the report to just those entries for the selected category or categories.

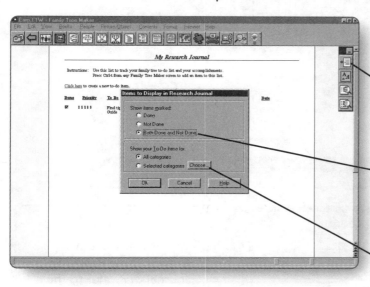

1. **Click** on the **Items to Display button**. The Items to Display in Research Journal dialog box will open.

2. **Click** on the **Both Done and Not Done option**. All items, whether done or not, will be included in the Research Journal.

3. **Click** on the **Choose button**. The Categories to Include dialog box will open. This dialog box is the same as many of the others you've seen. You simply select items from the Available categories list and place them in the Show items from these categories list.

4. **Click** on **OK**. The Categories to Include dialog box will close, saving the list of selected categories as they appear in the Show items from these categories list.

5. Click on **OK**. The Items to Display in Research Journal dialog box will close and the Research Journal will reflect your changes.

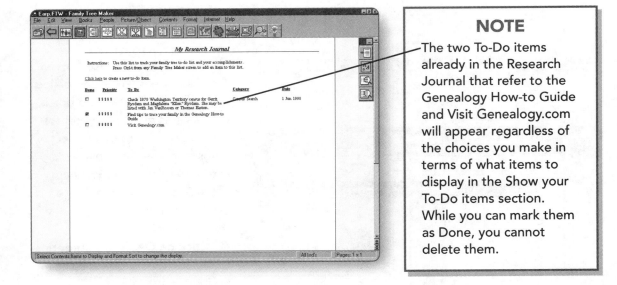

NOTE

The two To-Do items already in the Research Journal that refer to the Genealogy How-to Guide and Visit Genealogy.com will appear regardless of the choices you make in terms of what items to display in the Show your To-Do items section. While you can mark them as Done, you cannot delete them.

TIP

If you want to delete a To-Do item that you have created, you can do so by clicking on the item to highlight it and then pressing the Delete key.

23

Working with System Preferences

Family Tree Maker is a powerful program that offers many features and options. Better still, Family Tree Maker allows you, the user, to define your preferences for many of the screens and more common activities. In this chapter, you'll learn how to:

- Establish Fastfields
- Select screen labels for the Family Page
- Protect information about living relatives before sharing data
- Select FamilyFinder preferences
- Customize the toolbar buttons

Establishing Fastfields

One of the reasons why people use software programs in their genealogy research is to cut down on duplication. One of the ways Family Tree Maker aids in this is through the use of Fastfields.

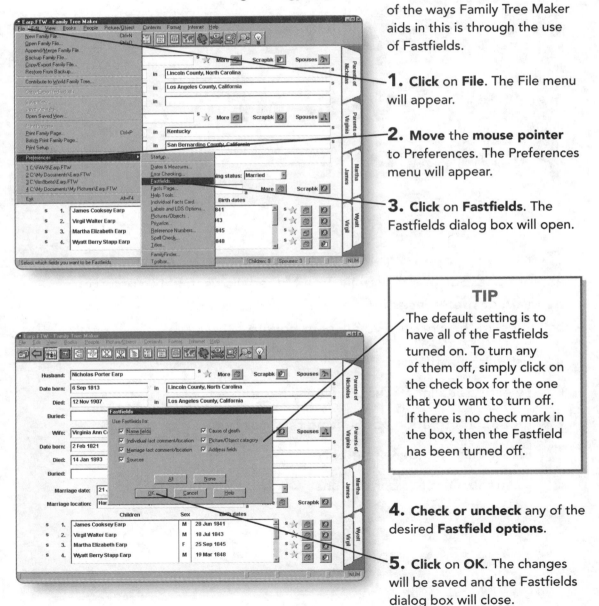

1. Click on **File**. The File menu will appear.

2. Move the **mouse pointer** to Preferences. The Preferences menu will appear.

3. Click on **Fastfields**. The Fastfields dialog box will open.

4. Check or uncheck any of the desired **Fastfield options**.

5. Click on **OK**. The changes will be saved and the Fastfields dialog box will close.

Selecting Family Page Labels

The default setting for the Family Page and the reports is Husband and Wife. Some people do not like to use these terms, instead preferring something like Father and Mother. Family Tree Maker allows you to make changes to these labels.

1. Click on **File**. The File menu will appear.

2. Move the **mouse pointer** to Preferences. The Preferences menu will appear.

3. Click on **Labels and LDS Options**. The Labels and LDS Options dialog box will open.

TIP

You can change one or all of the labels, or you can restore the default labels by clicking on the Reset labels to default button.

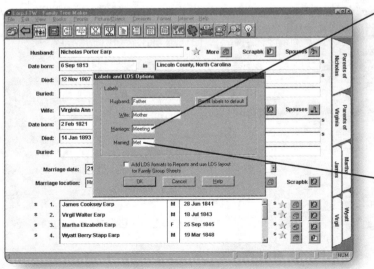

4. Type the **label name** in the Husband field. This will replace the word Husband on the Family Page and in reports.

5. Press the **Tab key**. The cursor will move to the Wife field.

6. Type the **label name** in the Wife field. This will replace the word Wife on the Family Page and in reports.

7. Press the **Tab key**. The cursor will move to the Marriage field.

8. Type the **label name** in the Marriage field. This will replace the word Marriage on the Family Page and in reports.

9. Press the **Tab key**. The cursor will move to the Married field.

10. Type the **label name** in the Married field. This will replace the word Married on the reports.

CAUTION
Making these changes will affect your entire Family File.

TIP
If you are a Latter-Day Saint or you prefer that style of Family Group Sheet, you might want to click on the Add LDS formats to Reports and use LDS layout for Family Group Sheets check box. When you do this, you disable the labels, because the LDS format has its own labels.

Protecting Privacy

There has been much concern of late, especially in the genealogical community, about the sharing of information on living individuals. Family Tree Maker allows you to privatize this information.

1. **Click** on **File**. The File menu will appear.

2. **Move** the **mouse pointer** to Preferences. The Preferences menu will appear.

3. **Click** on **Privatize**. The Privatize Information dialog box will open.

NOTE

The privatize option is intended as a temporary setting. It is designed to hide the Birth, Death, Marriage, More About Facts, Medical, and Notes information on living relatives.

4. **Click** on the **Privatize information check box**. A check mark will appear in the check box.

5. **Click** on **OK**. The Privatize Information dialog box will close.

Working with FamilyFinder Preferences

The FamilyFinder Report is a useful tool that lets you know of possible matching information on the Genealogy.com Web site or on the many Family Tree Maker CD-ROMs.

1. **Click** on **File**. The File menu will appear.

2. **Move** the **mouse pointer** to Preferences. The Preferences menu will appear.

3. **Click** on **FamilyFinder**. The FamilyFinder dialog box will open.

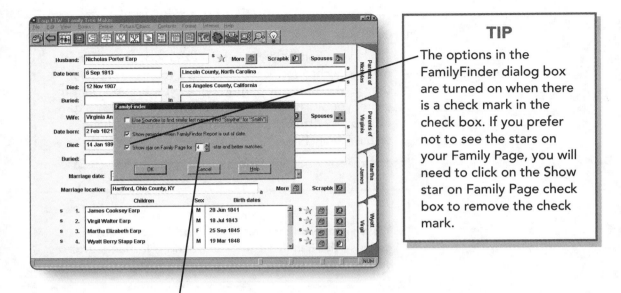

TIP

The options in the FamilyFinder dialog box are turned on when there is a check mark in the check box. If you prefer not to see the stars on your Family Page, you will need to click on the Show star on Family Page check box to remove the check mark.

NOTE

You can change the number of stars from 1 to 5 when including the stars on the Family Page. It is a good idea to use a higher setting because then you know that when there is a star, the FamilyFinder Report was a high match.

Customizing the Toolbar

While Family Tree Maker has set up the toolbar with those options that are considered the most popular, it is possible that you might rely more heavily on something not currently recognized on the toolbar. You can remove buttons, rearrange their order, and add new ones.

1. Click on **File**. The File menu will appear.

2. Move the **mouse pointer** to Preferences. The Preferences menu will appear.

3. Click on **Toolbar**. The Customize Toolbar dialog box will open.

4. Click on an **available item**. The item will be selected.

5. Click on the **inclusion button**. The item will be added to the bottom of the Your toolbar Contains list.

6. Click on the **newly added item** in the Your toolbar Contains list. The item will be selected.

7. Click on the **Move Up button**. The item will move up in the Your toolbar Contains list.

NOTE

The items that you move up and down in the Your toolbar Contains list will be moved to the left or right on the toolbar once you have finished making changes.

8. Click on **OK**. The Customize Toolbar dialog box will close and the toolbar will be updated.

NOTE

Notice that the toolbar now reflects the addition of the newly selected button.

24

Enhancing Your Family History Book

While the Book feature in Family Tree Maker offers many valuable options for creating a family history book, it is also possible to add additional reports and outside material to your book. In this chapter, you'll learn how to:

- Select additional reports in advance
- Use the Save View As option
- Rename the items in the Outline view
- Add place holders for outside material
- Add additional items to a previously saved book

Preparing Reports in Advance

People often do not think about the reports that they would like to include in their book until they are actually in the Books window. However, you can create specific reports ahead of time and then incorporate them into one or all of your books.

1. Press the **F2 key**. The Index of Individuals dialog box will open.

2. Type part of the **name** of the individual you want for the report. The highlight bar will move to the first person whose name contains those letters.

3. Click on the **individual** you want to select. That person will be highlighted.

4. Click on **OK**. The Index of Individuals dialog box will close.

Selecting and Formatting Reports

You must first decide the goal of these additional reports. For instance, do you want a chapter of Family Group Sheets on each family that will be found in the narrative section of the book?

1. Click on the **Family Group Sheet button**. The Family Group Sheet for the individual you selected will appear.

TIP

If you are going to create a chapter of Family Group Sheets in your book, you might want to change the generic "Family Group Sheet" title on each Family Group Sheet Report you generate to better represent the individuals included in the report.

2. Click on **Contents**. The Contents menu will appear.

3. Click on **Title & Footnote**. The Title & Footnote for Family Group Sheet dialog box will open.

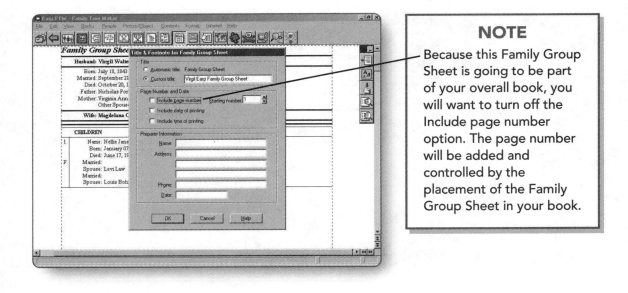

4. Click on the **Custom title radio button**. The cursor will move to the Custom title field.

5. Type the **new title** for the Family Group Sheet.

TIP

You might want to use the name of the father as your title if you will be creating many Family Group Sheets for your book.

NOTE

Because this Family Group Sheet is going to be part of your overall book, you will want to turn off the Include page number option. The page number will be added and controlled by the placement of the Family Group Sheet in your book.

6. Click in the **Name field**. The cursor will move to the Name field.

7. Type the **name** of the preparer and **press** the **Tab key**. The cursor will move to the first Address field.

TIP

Because this is going to be included in your book, you might not want to include your address at the bottom of each page. However, don't overlook this valuable information when printing out Family Group Sheets to share with other researchers.

NOTE

The preparer name, address, and phone number will print at the bottom of the Family Group Sheet. However, the date will print at the top, opposite the title.

8. Click on **OK**. The Title & Footnote for Family Group Sheet dialog box will close and the changes will take effect on the Family Group Sheet Report that is displayed.

Using the Save View As Option

Once you have your report just the way you want it, you can save the report and use it later on in any of your books.

1. Click on **File**. The File menu will appear.

2. Click on **Save Family Group Sheet As**. The Save View As dialog box will open.

NOTE

This File menu option will change according to the report you have open.

---

3. Type the **name** of the report. The default name will be changed for the title that appears in the View list.

4. Click on **OK**. The Save View As dialog box will close.

TIP
You can always make changes to any saved view. The Open Saved View option in the File menu reopens the view, allowing you to make the changes.

5. Click on the appropriate **view**. The view will be highlighted.

6. Click on the **Open button**. The Open Saved View dialog box will close and the selected Report view will open.

Renaming Outline Items

While Family Tree Maker has default names for all of the reports, you are not required to use those titles.

1. Click on **Books**. The Books menu will appear.

2. Click on **Open Book**. The Open Book dialog box will open.

3. Click on the appropriate **book**. The book will be highlighted.

4. Click on **OK**. The Open Book dialog box will close and the Books view will open.

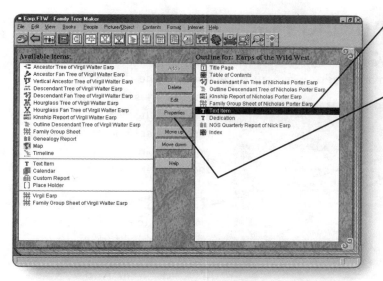

5. Click on the appropriate **item** in the Outline for list. The item will be highlighted.

6. Click on the **Properties button**. The Item Properties dialog box will open.

7. Type the new **name** in the Item name field. This will replace the old item name.

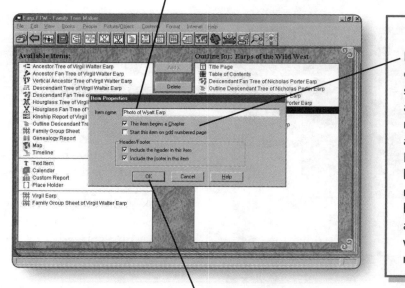

TIP

In the Item Properties dialog box, you can also set up chapter beginnings and control whether or not the report begins on an odd-numbered page. If the report is going to begin a new chapter, you might want to think about beginning that chapter on an odd-numbered page, which is the standard in most books.

8. Click on **OK**. The Item Properties dialog box will close and the item name will change in the Outline for list.

Adding Place Holders

Many times you will want to incorporate a family story created in another program, or some special hand-drawn charts or photo pages in your book. The place holder allows you to reserve a set number of pages anywhere in your book to insert these other items after printing.

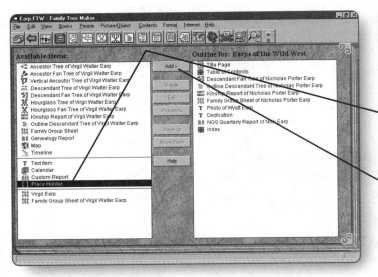

1. Click on **Place Holder** in the Available items list. Place Holder will be highlighted.

2. Click on the **Add button**. The Place Holder Properties dialog box will open.

3. Type the **name** of the item in the Item name field. The words "Place Holder" will be replaced by the name you have typed.

TIP

You will want to give the place holder a descriptive name so that you can easily recall what will go into those pages. This item name will be displayed in the Outline for list and, unlike in the other reports, you cannot open this item to refresh your memory about what is in it.

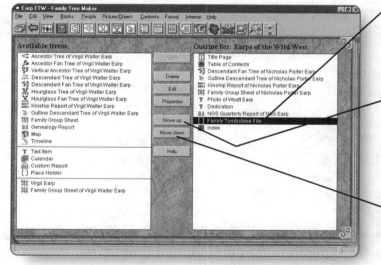

4. Click on the **up or down arrows** to select the number of pages to hold.

5. Click on **OK**. The Place Holder Properties dialog box will close.

6. Click on the **place holder item** in the Outline for list. The place holder item will be highlighted.

7a. Click on the **Move up button**. The place holder item will be moved up in the Outline for list.

OR

7b. Click on the **Move down button**. The place holder item will be moved down in the Outline for list.

NOTE

Don't forget that the Index must be the last item in the Outline for list. In fact, if you try to move something below it, Family Tree Maker will open a message box explaining that you cannot do that.

Adding to a Book

While you may have already created a book and saved it, that does not mean you can't build on that book. Family Tree Maker allows you to add additional reports at a later date to any previously saved book.

Adding Saved Reports to Books

You can incorporate Save View As reports into any book at any time. Once you have created them, they are available in any Books view, whether new or previously saved.

1. Click on **Books**. The Books menu will appear.

2. Click on **Open Book**. The Open Book dialog box will open.

3. Click on the appropriate **book**. The book will be highlighted.

4. Click on **OK**. The Open Book dialog box will close and the Books view will open.

NOTE

The previously saved reports will always appear at the bottom of the Available items list.

5. Click on the appropriate **saved report** in the Available items list. The report will be highlighted.

6. Click on the **Add button**. The report will be added to the Outline for list.

NOTE

At this point, the saved report can be repositioned or edited like the other items in the Outline for list.

7. Click on the **Edit button**. The report will open for editing.

8. Click on the **Go Back button** when you are done editing the report. You will be returned to the Books view.

NOTE

You can see the page number that has been assigned based on where the report is presently in the order of the book. This number will change if the report is moved up or down in the Outline for list in the Books view.

Adding Reports about Other Individuals

When a book is first created, it relies on the reports of the selected individual. Once a book has been saved, though, you can add additional reports about other people, giving you a lot of flexibility in your book and its layout.

1. Press the **F2 key**. The Index of Individuals dialog box will open.

2. Click on the desired **individual**. The individual will be highlighted.

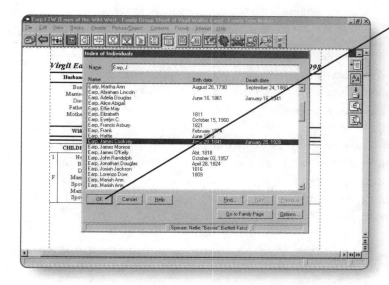

3. Click on **OK**. The Index of Individuals dialog box will close and the Available items list in the Books view will reflect the change in individuals.

4. Click on the appropriate **item** in the Available items list. That item will be highlighted.

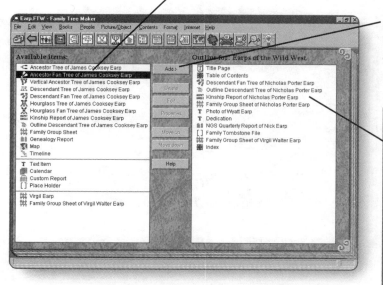

5. Click on the **Add button**. The selected item will be added to the bottom of the Outline for list, just above the Index item.

TIP

If you click on the selected item in the Outline for list, you can use the various buttons to reposition the item, edit it, or change its properties. It is now a part of the book unless you elect to delete it.

> **NOTE**
>
> Notice that while you changed the focus of the individual in the Available items list, your saved reports are still available.

You have not only been introduced to Family Tree Maker, but you have also been shown many of the advanced features and some tricks to get the most out of the program. Sharing your genealogy online or in print is limited only by your own possibilities. Happy ancestor hunting!

Part VI Review Questions

1. What happens when you change the Beginning status of a marriage on the Family Page? *See "Getting Family Page and More About Marriage Facts to Work Together" in Chapter 20*

2. How do you remove a custom fact name that you created? *See "Removing a Custom Fact Name" in Chapter 20*

3. Can you export your Family File to a GEDCOM file? *See "Creating a GEDCOM File" in Chapter 21*

4. How do you open another Family File? *See "Opening a Different Family File" in Chapter 21*

5. What are the four ways you can search for individuals to add to a Custom Report? *See "Using the Find Button to Include Individuals in the Custom Report" in Chapter 22*

6. How can you find To-Do items that deal with a specific resource or repository? *See "Selecting To-Do Categories" in Chapter 22*

7. Can you protect information on living individuals in your Family File? *See "Protecting Privacy" in Chapter 23*

8. How do you add another button to the toolbar in Family Tree Maker? *See "Customizing the Toolbar" in Chapter 23*

9. Can you create individual reports to include in your family history book? *See "Preparing Reports in Advance" in Chapter 24*

10. How do you add reports on a new person to a previously saved book? *See "Adding to a Book" in Chapter 24*

PART VII

Appendixes

A

Installing Family Tree Maker

Family Tree Maker has been designed to be easy to install. In this appendix, you'll learn how to:

- Install Family Tree Maker Version 9 on your computer
- Choose the options you want to install
- Uninstall Family Tree Maker from your computer

Installing Family Tree Maker Version 9

Most computers use an autorun feature when you put a new program CD into your CD-ROM drive—the CD begins to run without your having to do anything.

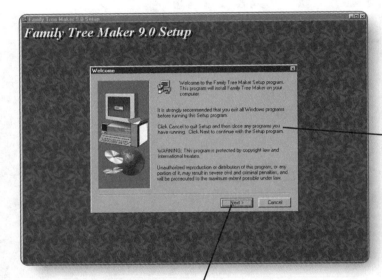

1. Insert the **Family Tree Maker 9 CD-ROM** into your computer's CD-ROM drive. The automatic installer will start.

> **NOTE**
>
> Family Tree Maker's installer will encourage you to close any programs you have running at the time you begin to install Family Tree Maker 9. (This is a good idea whenever you are installing software.)

2. Click on **Next** after you have closed all other open programs. The Software License Agreement dialog box will open.

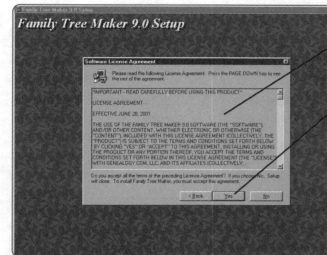

3. Read the **License Agreement**.

4. Click on **Yes**. The Choose Destination Location dialog box will open.

TIP

Usually the suggested Destination Folder is the most appropriate one. However, if you do not like where the installer is going to place Family Tree Maker, click on the Browse button and select another directory.

5. Click on **Next**. The Select Components dialog box will open.

Choosing Components

Family Tree Maker allows you to decide which of the available components you want to install.

1. Click on the **check box** next to the components you want to install. A check mark will appear next to each component you select.

NOTE

After you select a component, its size will be shown to the right of it, and the Space Required total will reflect the change.

2. If you want to install only some of the ClickArt and/or Maps, **click** on **Change**. The Select Sub-components dialog box will open.

3. Click on the **sub-components** that you don't want to install. The check marks next to the sub-components you click on will be removed.

4. Click on **Continue**. The Select Sub-components dialog box will close.

5. Click on **Next**. The Select Program Folder dialog box will open.

6a. Type a **program folder name** if you do not want to use the one supplied by Family Tree Maker.

OR

6b. Select a **folder** from those already listed. The folder will be highlighted.

7. Click on **Next**. The program will be installed. Family Tree Maker will then look for your browser software, to use when you go online from within the program.

8. Select your **browser** and then **click** on **Next**. The final screen appear.

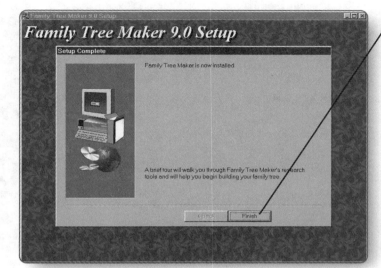

9. Click on the **Finish button** to complete the installation process.

Uninstalling Family Tree Maker

There might come a time when you need to remove Family Tree Maker from your computer. Family Tree Maker has included an uninstall option.

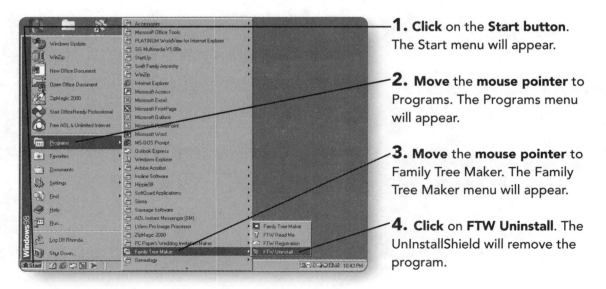

1. Click on the **Start button**. The Start menu will appear.

2. Move the **mouse pointer** to Programs. The Programs menu will appear.

3. Move the **mouse pointer** to Family Tree Maker. The Family Tree Maker menu will appear.

4. Click on **FTW Uninstall**. The UnInstallShield will remove the program.

B

Using Keyboard Shortcuts

Many people prefer not to have to reach for the mouse when they're entering information. Keyboard shortcuts allow you to accomplish many of the tasks for which you would normally need to use the mouse. Throughout the book your attention has been called to some of the keyboard shortcuts included in this appendix, but here you can see the information at a glance. In this appendix, you'll learn how to:

- Use the keyboard shortcuts found in Family Tree Maker
- Use keyboard combinations in text windows

Learning the Keyboard Shortcuts

While it might seem like you will never remember the shortcuts, you will find that they become second nature as you spend more time in Family Tree Maker.

Getting Help

Although you can always open the Help menu, you can use the keyboard shortcuts shown in the following table to get to the help you need more quickly.

To execute this command	Do this
Use Family Tree Maker Help	Press the F1 key
Use the What's This? button	Press the Shift and F1 keys at the same time (Shift+F1)

Working in Family Tree Maker

The following table puts the keyboard shortcuts related to Family Tree Maker commands together for an easy reference.

To execute this command	Do this
Create a new Family File	Press Ctrl+N
Open a different Family File	Press Ctrl+O
Print a report	Press Ctrl+P
Create a new To-Do item	Press Ctrl+T
Access the Index of Individuals	Press F2
View a source	Press Ctrl+S
Open the Other Spouses dialog box	Press F3
Access a More About Picture window	Press Ctrl+M
Get Family File status	Press Alt+F1
Get system information	Press Ctrl+F1
Exit Family Tree Maker	Press Alt+F4

Working with Text

While most of the entries in Family Tree Maker are made in fields, there are a number of text windows for typing notes. The following tables contain some shortcuts you might find useful when working in the text windows.

Selecting Text

The first step in manipulating your text is to select it. The following table offers some keyboard combinations for selecting a letter, a word, a line, or more.

To execute this command	Do this
Highlight the character to the right of the insertion point	Press Shift+Right Arrow
Highlight the character to the left of the insertion point	Press Shift+Left Arrow
Highlight an entire word to the right of the insertion point	Press Ctrl+Shift+Right Arrow
Highlight an entire word to the left of the insertion point	Press Ctrl+Shift+Left Arrow
Highlight an entire line	Press Shift+End
Highlight a paragraph one line at a time	Press Shift+Down Arrow for each line of the paragraph
Highlight all lines above the insertion point	Press Ctrl+Shift+Home

Copying and Pasting Text

After you select the text you want to work with, you might want to remove it or copy it for placement elsewhere. The following table contains the keyboard combinations you need to manipulate selected text.

To execute this command	Do this
Copy text	Press Ctrl+C
Cut text	Press Ctrl+X
Paste text	Press Ctrl+V
Delete text	Press Del

Glossary

A

Ahnentafel. German for *ancestor table*. In addition to being a chart, it also refers to a genealogical numbering system.

Ancestor. A person from whom one descends.

Ancestor Tree. Also known as a *Pedigree Chart,* this chart begins with a specific individual and displays direct lineage of all of the individual's ancestors.

Annotation. Personal notes or comments that either explain or critique. Family Tree Maker employs annotations in the Bibliography Report.

B

Bibliography. A report that shows a list of sources used to compile the information included in the genealogy. The sources follow an accepted format, which Family Tree Maker has built into the program.

BMP. Bitmap. A file format for graphics.

Book. In Family Tree Maker, a compilation of reports generated for a family or an individual, including family trees, miscellaneous reports, stories, photos, a table of contents, and an index.

Browser. See *Web Browser*.

C

Case Sensitive. Differentiating between uppercase and lowercase characters.

Citation. The accepted notation of the source of information.

Cite. The act of making note of the proof that supports a conclusion or claimed fact in the genealogy.

Clipboard. A memory feature of the Windows environment that allows a person to copy or cut text or graphics from one document and paste them into another.

D

Descendant. A person who descends lineally from another.

Descendant Tree. A chart that lists an individual and his or her descendants.

E

Endnotes. Source citations and explanatory notes that appear at the end of a document, specifically a tree or report.

Export. To transfer data from one computer to another or from one computer program to another.

F

Family File. Family Tree Maker's name for the database that contains the information about your lineage.

FamilyFinder Index. A genealogical list containing over 750 million names that is included in Family Tree Maker's CDs and online.

Family Group Sheet. A form that displays information on a single, complete family unit.

Family Page. The main screen in Family Tree Maker, into which you enter information about a particular individual and family.

Fastfields. Family Tree Maker remembers the names of the last 50 locations you have typed in so that as you begin to type in a place in a new location field, Family Tree Maker shows you possible matches based on the letters you have typed up to that point.

Format. One of Family Tree Maker's options for developing the style and look of reports and trees.

G

GEDCOM. GEnealogical Data COMmunication. A standard designed by the Family History Department of the Church of Jesus Christ of Latter-Day Saints for transferring data between different genealogy software packages.

Genealogy Report. A narrative style report that details a family through one or more generations and includes basic facts about each member in addition to biographical information that was entered through Family Tree Maker.

Generation. The period of time between the birth of one group of individuals and the next—usually about 25 to 33 years.

GIF. Graphic Interchange Format. A graphic file format that is widely used in Web page documents.

Given Name. The first name (and middle name) given to a child at birth or at his or her baptism. Also known as a *Christian name*.

H

Home Page. The main page of a Web site.

Hourglass Tree. A chart showing both the ancestors and the descendants of a selected individual. When printed, the tree resembles an hourglass because the ancestors spread out above the selected individual and the descendants spread out below.

HTML. Hypertext Markup Language. The standard language for creating and formatting Web pages.

I

Import. To bring into a program a file that was created using another program.

Individual Facts Card. A multi-tabbed dialog box that allows you easy access to all of the personal information (corresponding to the Family Page and More About pages) for a specific individual.

Inline Notes. The sources that appear within the text as opposed to at the bottom or end of a page in Family Tree Maker's Genealogy Reports.

K

Kinship. In genealogy, this refers to the relationship between one individual and any or all of his or her relatives. This can be displayed through the Kinship Report in Family Tree Maker.

J

JPEG. Joint Photographic Expert Group. Graphics that use the .jpg extension include a compression technique that reduces the size of the graphics file.

M

Maternal Ancestor. An ancestor on the mother's side of the family.

N

NGSQ. *National Genealogical Society Quarterly*. A periodical published by that society. Also refers to the NGS Quarterly numbering system offered in descending genealogy reports.

O

OLE. Object Linking and Embedding. A technology that allows you to create items in one program and place them in another, including video clips, still images, pictures, word-processing files, and spreadsheet files.

Outline Descendant Tree. A chart that shows in an indented outline format an individual's children, grandchildren, great-grandchildren, and so on through the generations.

P

Paternal Ancestor. An ancestor on the father's side of the family.

Pedigree Chart. A chart that shows the direct ancestors of an individual. Known in Family Tree Maker as an *Ancestor Tree*.

Preferred. A term Family Tree Maker uses in reference to parents, spouses, or duplicate events, meaning that you want to see that selection first or have it displayed in trees and reports.

Primary Individual. The main individual in any of the Family Tree Maker charts or reports.

R

Register. Refers to the descending genealogy format used by the New England Historic Genealogical Society. This also refers to their periodical of the same name.

Reports. Any of a number of standard and custom displays in various formats that Family Tree Maker can create.

Research Journal. A record used by genealogists to keep track of their research findings and tasks to be accomplished.

RTF. Rich Text Format. A cross-platform, cross-application text document format. It retains some of the formatting information that is supported by many word processors.

S

Scrapbook. The term used by Family Tree Maker for the collections of photographs, images, video, sound, and OLE objects that can be stored for each individual and marriage in the Family File.

Siblings. Children of the same parents.

Source. The record, such as a book, an e-mail message, or an interview, from which specific information was obtained.

Spouse. The person to whom another person is married.

Surname. The family name or last name of an individual.

T

Tree. The term Family Tree Maker uses to refer to its various charts. See *Ancestor Tree*, *Descendant Tree*, and *Outline Descendant Tree*.

U

URL. Uniform Resource Locator. The address used by a Web browser to locate a page on the Web.

W

WAV. Windows Audio Visual. The sound files that work with Media Player and Sound Recorder.

Web Browser. The software that lets you access pages on the Web. The browser reads the HTML code and converts it to the pictures, colors, menu options, and overall design that you view on your monitor.

Web Page. A document on the Internet that is written using a scripting language such as HTML.

Web Site. A location on the Internet maintained by a single individual, company, or entity that provides information, graphics, and other items.

World Family Tree (WFT) Project. A multi-volume CD collection created by Genealogy.com from the genealogies submitted electronically by family history enthusiasts and indexed in the FamilyFinder Index.

World Wide Web. A graphical interface that is composed of Internet sites that provide researchers with access to documents and other files.

Index

World Family Tree Collection

- Features hundreds of thousands of actual family trees.
- View them online, or download them to your desktop.

Grow Your Family Tree With This Data:
Finding one ancestor in a World Family Tree can instantly add entire branches to your family tree. View a tree online, or download it to your computer using our quick and easy wizard. At a glance, you'll see family relationships and details of vital events. It's the fastest way to add information to your own family research.

View Family Trees Online:
Now, you can instantly view pedigrees online with World Family Tree. Just click on the "view" option and you will access the family tree. (sample below)

Easy to Download:
Or if you'd like, you can download a family tree directly in Family Tree Maker using the recently released auto-installer. The auto-installer is an install "wizard" that allows you to point and click to execute a no-nonsense download of any pedigree from World Family Tree.

Order toll-free by phone: 1-800-548-1806
- OR-
Order online at http://www.familytreemaker.com/wftonline/

Genealogy Library Subscription

The most comprehensive resource for discovering your family history.

Fill in your family tree with your unique story:
When you're researching your family tree, it's important to know that Great-Great Uncle Charlie married on January 12th, 1872. But it's fascinating to uncover the guest list, what his bride wore, and the traditions they celebrated. Discover those details and more with Genealogy Library.

Genealogy Library is a growing collection of relevant and historically significant data: U.S. focused sources confirming information in your family tree, giving you links to further research, and adding the flavor that makes research compelling.

With a subscription to Genealogy Library you'll receive:

- More than 3,200 genealogy books, including more than 1,900 genealogies, 250 town and county histories, 900 vital records collections and 283,000 images from the 1850 census.

- Census images from 22 of the 34 states covered by the 1850 census.

- More than 50 collections of historical records.

Genealogical Records: Early Texas Settlers 1700s-1800s

Texas Society, Colonial Dames of 17th Century, Ancestor Lineages, Page 221

Previous Image | Next Image | First Page   My Online Data Library
Save This Image | View Image for Printing

#7860 Ruth Willey Haynes

WILLEY, ISAAC IV b 18 Sept 1699, Lyme, CT, d 2 June 1767, Lyme, CT; m 12 May 1727, New London, CT, Deliverance Tolman, b 1705, d 12 Nov 1763, Lyme, CT
SERVICE: Freeman 1753, landowner; CT
CHILDREN:
1. Nathaniel b 12 Feb 1727
2. Deliverance b 8 Jan 1728;
   m Mr. Allan
3. Abigail b 18 May 1732, d.y.
* 4. Barzillai b 10 Sept 1734, Lyme, CT, m Joanna Church, d bef 1760, Lyme, CT
5. Darius b 3 May 1737; m Mary Willey
6. Miriam m Daniel Atwood
7. Abigail bapt 6 Oct 1745
8. Comfort bapt 4 June 1749
#7860 Ruth Willey Haynes

WILLEY, JOHN Lt. b 1642, New London, CT, d 2 May 1688, Haddam, CT; m 18 Mar 1688, Miriam Moore
SERVICE: King Philip's War, landowner 1696, military; CT
CHILDREN:
* 1. Isaac b 18 Jan 1670, New London, CT; m 14 Dec 1697, New London, CT, Rose Bennett
2. Isabel b 31 Oct 1663

WILLIAMS, JOHN b m 1620, Eng, d VA; m bef 1645, VA
SERVICE: Landowner, cattleman; VA
CHILDREN:
* 1. John Sr. b 1645, York Co., VA d aft 1685, York Co, VA; m 1655, (See "Widow" Williams)
2. Edward
3. Obediah
4. Richard
5. William
#11954 Minnie Harrington Henderson

WILLIAMS, JOHN b ca 1640, d 1880, VA; m 2. Eve --, d 7705, Richmond Co., VA
SERVICE: Landowner, Rappahannock; VA
CHILDREN: By Eve
* 1. Katherine b ca 1670; m Abraham Goad
#16535 Irene Ewing Hoss Bachner

WILLIAMS, JOHN b ca 1640, Eng. or Wales, d (will) 9 Mar 1601, Isle of Wight Co., VA; m ca 1660, VA, Anne --, b m 1645, Eng. or VA, d aft 1694
SERVICE: Transporter 1633, juror 1697; VA
CHILDREN:
1. John
2. Theophilus
* 3. William

Order toll-free by phone: 1-800-548-1806

- OR-

Order online at http://www.familytreemaker.com/_glc_

Data Collections

Five Convenient Options for Finding Your Ancestors from Home

Find Family with Data Resources

Find the essential details you need to quickly grow your family tree. Using our vast data collections, you'll discover more of your family story, whether you're just getting started or an avid researcher.

Genealogy Library
Your premiere family-finding resource ó a comprehensive online tool.
A far-reaching collection of sources sure to expand your family story - explore everything from family histories to marriage data to military records.

World Family Tree
Expand your family tree with the largest pedigree database available.
Are you a new or veteran researcher? Either way, you can quickly add entire branches to your family tree and work with others in your family line.

1900 Census
The best source for your American family's turn-of-the-century story.
Make new connections beyond your family's word-of-mouth history. Search nearly 75 million people in the only resource designed to list everyone in 1900 America.

International & Passenger Records
The right resource for tracing ancestors across the seas and beyond.
If you're ready to research family history overseas, start here. You'll travel from hard-to-find international sources to the port of U.S. entry with this online resource.

Data on CD
If you prefer to research using CD-ROM, Genealogy.com Data CD-ROMs provide easy and convenient access to incredibly rich data sources.

- Fully guaranteed and packed with everything from vital records to passenger lists, these CDs bring your family history to life.

- 309 titles and growing, these are hard-to-locate resources previously available only through distant libraries, private collections, and dusty used-book stores.

1900 Census Collection

Genealogy.com's **1900 Census Subscription** is your one resource for indexed and fully searchable, high quality United States Census microfilm images —an essential resource for any American genealogist.

- Discover this critical, bridging resource —most of the 1890 U.S. Census burned by a fire in 1921.
- Search or browse easily by head of household across 75 million names.
- Access data for the entire U.S., including the District of Columbia, the Indian territories and the military.
- Flexible pricing lets you choose monthly or annual online access.

America in 1900 was a place of invention, discovery, and promise.
Subscribe today and discover details of your family's story during this dynamic period of American history from a single research destination.

Order online at http://www.familytreemaker.com/1900census.html

---

International & Passenger Records Collection

With the **International and Passenger Records Collection**, you get a dynamic online resource for reaching your immigrant ancestors.

- Quick online searching across **FIVE CENTURIES** of data.
- High quality, often hard-to-find sources including passenger lists, international census data, land records, and more.
- Research U.S. Immigration, Western Europe, and Britain.
- Instant, anytime access to more than 13 million records.
- Available via monthly or yearly subscriptions.
- As our collection grows, yours does too.

Order online at http://www.familytreemaker.com/internationalsub.html

---

Order toll-free by phone: 1-800-548-1806